From Redundancy to Employment

From Redundancy to Employment

The Must Have Guide and How to Answer Those Killer Interview Questions

Doreen Yarnold

Specialist in Business and Life Solutions

All rights reserved. This material is copyright protected.

Published By:

DAY-Begley Publishing
128 Elmdon Lane
Marston Green
Birmingham
B37 7EG

Copyright: Doreen Yarnold – All Rights Reserved
Publication Date: February 2009

LEGAL NOTICES

DAY-Begley Publishing and its successors or assigns (collectively, the 'Publisher') owns all right, title, and interest to this publication. No part of this publication may be reproduced, distributed, or transmitted in any form, in whole or in part, or by any means, mechanical or electronic, including photocopying or recording, or transmitted by email, without the express permission from the Publisher.

You have no rights to sell, reprint, reproduce or digitize this Report. All attempts have been made to verify information provided in this publication. Neither the author nor the Publisher assumes any responsibility for errors, omissions, or contrary interpretation of the subject matter herein.

This publication is not intended for use as a source of any advice such as legal, medical, or accounting. The Publisher wants to stress that the information contained herein may be subject to varying international federal state and/or local laws of regulation. The purchaser or reader of this publication assumes responsibility for the use of these materials and information. Adherence to all applicable laws and regulations governing professional licensing, business practices, advertising and all other aspects of doing business in the United Kingdom, Europe, US, and Canada or any other jurisdiction is the sole responsibility or liability of the purchaser or reader. Neither the author nor the Publisher assume any responsibility or liability whatsoever on the behalf of any purchaser or reader of these materials. Any perceived slight of specific people or organisation is unintentional.

How to Get the Best from this Book

A Book of Two Parts

This book has been compiled for people who have experienced or are currently going through a redundancy situation. It is written in two parts – Part 1 and Part 2. Part 1 will only take about an hour or so to read, and therefore is also ideal for those people who are about to attend interviews imminently. Part 2 is for those people with a little more time to explore the whole subject of securing employment a little further.

You can do a lot of preparation in a relatively short period of time provided you are focused and engaged in the process. From page 41 you'll find some of the more difficult questions interviewers ask. I will take you through some hot tips and techniques for answering these killer questions together with lots of sample answers, so that you can actually see how to structure your answer for maximum effect. Difficult questions can sometimes knock you completely off your stride at interview, and a clumsy or ill-considered answer can blow your chances of getting the job you want.

Part 1 - Contents:

Coping with rejection	*11*
Shaping Your CV	*13*
General CV Structure and Format	*21*
The Interview – Overview	*27*
The Interview Structure	*31*
Those Killer Interview Questions	*43*
Questions that should not be asked at Interview	*81*
Creating Impact	*87*
Body Language	*88*
The way you say what you say	*91*
The words that you use	*91*
The Clothes That You Wear	*94*
Personal Grooming	*95*

Part 2 – Contents:

Your rights and entitlements under Redundancy	*103*
Writing your covering letter	*113*
The recruitment structure	*121*
Telephone Interview	*121*
First Interview	*123*
Final Interview	*124*
Panel Interview	*125*
Psychometric testing	*129*
Assessment activities	*133*
The inexperienced interviewer	*149*
Confidence	*151*
Assertiveness	*175*
Marketing yourself	*181*

Preface

Well let's just start by acknowledging how you're likely to be feeling right now. Being made redundant is an awful process to have to go through, and you can be forgiven for allowing yourself a certain amount of time to get to grips with it all, and to get your head around it.

Depending upon how long you've been out of work, you could be feeling anything from devastated and shocked, if it's only recently happened, right through to feeling down and depressed if it happened a while ago, and anything in between.

The emotions attached to redundancy are many fold and can also include anger, resentment (why me?), failure (I must be a loser), disillusion, frustration, panic, to name but a few - This is perfectly normal, and whilst it may be of no consequence at all, most people who experience redundancy go through some or all of these emotional states.

The key difference between those who go on to gain employment in the future and those who don't is 100%

down to your state of mind. Let me explain. When life throws a curve-ball which it does to all of us from time to time – no-one on this planet is exempt from this, we have a choice. We can't stop these things from happening, but we do have a choice as to how we react and respond to them. You can choose either to let it crush you, or you can see it for what it is, a distressing event that you can get through if you adopt the right attitude and mindset.

Please forgive me it is not my intention to patronise, only to help, and I know that you may not want to hear what I'm saying right now but I promise you, what you're feeling right now will pass. You may even emerge stronger and wiser for the experience.

As awful as redundancy is, it isn't life threatening. I'm trusting that the fact that you are reading this book means that you have already made the choice to take some practical steps towards your future, and this is where I can help you.

The reason I wrote this book in two parts is that in the circumstance of being made redundant, I cannot imagine that your first inclination is to sit down and read a whole book, no matter how useful it might be, so Part 1 is the key areas to focus on first, will only take you about an hour or so to read, and contains most if not all of the techniques and strategies you will need to at least get you moving in the right direction quickly.

Biography

Doreen Yarnold is one of the UKs leading insights on Leadership, Management and Business development including Recruitment and Interviewing skills. She is also an Executive Coach and Mentor and specialises in helping businesses achieve their key objectives.

Doreen has been training managers to recruit and interview for the past 12 years, and latterly from within her own business: It's About Results which she started in 2004.

An extensive commercial career heading up numerous large businesses has provided Doreen with significant and valuable experience. She knows what it takes for a business to be successful, and she knows what it takes for a person to be successful. Her love of sharing knowledge and helping people live their best life is what credibility amongst her peers.

Doreen Yarnold, the founder of 'It's About Results' has been intimately involved with Leadership Training and Business Growth consultancy for the past twelve years. It is an inherent passion that drives her to support people and businesses to achieve Measurable Results. Doreen's ongoing research and studies of this incredibly exciting subject keeps her and her company at the leading edge of Leadership and Business Growth development.

Having spent many years in senior corporate positions running multiple-site businesses for large companies she gained broad commercial expertise and knowledge of what makes businesses successful and how to turn a failing business around from loss into significant profit.

Much of her work is spent working with such businesses, helping and supporting the management teams through the sometimes painful change processes required to make lasting and sustained transformations of their business.

Doreen's overriding passion is people and helping them develop both their business skills and their life skills – this book supports both of these goals.

Coping With Rejection

In recessionary times such as these, even the very best of candidates is unlikely to get the first job they go after. Because there are so many more people after the same job, you will have to get used to the fact that you will be rejected for a number of the jobs you go for. Learn to see rejection as a learning experience. What did you learn about yourself and about the process; how well did you answer the questions; where could you improve next time; were there any questions asked that you didn't anticipate – if so write them down to help with preparation for the next interview.

If you can try to see rejection as being one step further towards the job you will eventually get, it will keep you motivated and mentally on top of your game. There will be lots of de-motivated people out there all applying for the same jobs as you, but if you are the one with the positive outlook who comes across at interview as a motivated, well prepared, well groomed and credible candidate, you will stand out for all the right reasons, and with any luck help you land that job.

If you want further coaching/mentoring support through this difficult phase of your life, please call me, Doreen Yarnold on: 07903-810808.

Getting Through the CV Sifting Process

Shaping Your CV

This doesn't mean you should lie and embellish your CV to give a false impression, merely a restructuring and possible rewording to capture the essence of what you believe the Company is looking for. For example, most companies structure all roles against a set of desired competencies which they believe a prospective candidate should have in order to be able to undertake their role to an acceptable standard. Getting to know what these competencies are for the role you wish to apply for, has to be your first mission so that you can shape your CV appropriately, and stand the best chance of getting an interview. We will cover a little later how you can also use these to prepare for the interview. This is the most powerful method of ensuring you get short-listed for any job, but you won't find these nuggets in any text book.

Now some organisations see it as a real positive if a prospective candidate calls up to ask for a role profile so that they can assess whether the role is appropriate for them or not, so don't be concerned about asking for it. Once you have this, it should be pretty evident what competencies they are looking for. You can then shape your CV so that some of these competencies are 'woven in' to the fabric of your content. Not overtly, but subtly, enough to ensure that your CV at least gets through the filter process. If you can't get hold of a Role Profile, you will need to use the information you glean from your research of the company to try to establish the company mission and values and weave these into your CV.

The more knowledge you have about the Company and the proposed vacancy at CV stage the more likely you will be to gain that all important competitive edge. If the Company is big on people, and again you may be able to get this from their web site (Investors in People etc) and their accompanying blurb, you should try to ensure you bring this element into the content of your CV so that this is evident to whoever is doing the sifting.

You are effectively looking to tick as many of their boxes as possible. At this stage your sole intention is to get through the sifting stage and get an invitation to an interview. Remember though, you must be able to back this up at interview. If you lie or embellish, a skilled interviewer will likely uncover this at the interview, so be careful on this one.

In terms of structure, as an absolute minimum you need the following:

- **Your Personal Details**

    Name, address, telephone numbers (inc. Mobile number), email address. It is also good practice, although not essential, to include marital status, nationality, and whether you hold a full & clean driving licence. If you do it's worth putting it in, if not, keep it out at this stage.

- **Personal Profile**

    This is essentially your headline statement, your hook to entice the reader to read all of your CV and encourage them to pay attention to your content. When you've read and digested this report in its entirety your content will absolutely deserve to be paid some attention, as it will be compelling and powerful.

- **Career and Work Experience**

    This needs to run in chronological order, and *always* starting with your most recent positions first. You will need to be as comprehensive as possible in terms of the company details such as name, address, telephone number, and web site address for each company listed. Then a brief summary of your key responsibilities and achievements in each role (this is where you can bring in some of those key competencies), so that the sifter can more easily match you to their job criteria. Be succinct here, but not *so* much that you skimp on important information.

- **Education**

A good idea here is to first list your professional education first (if you hold professional qualifications) together with grades achieved. Again, these need to be in chronological order. Then you can list your school and college education and qualification details in the same way. If you don't have any qualification don't worry, just complete the details of your school. If specific qualifications are required you will risk not get through the sifting process, however, you should still apply but attaching a great covering letter that outlines your experience. If it is compelling enough and well written, it may just be enough to get you through to Interview.

- **Key Skills and Competencies**

    This is a great section to include on CV, and makes the job of the CV sifter even easier to match you against their criteria. List all of the skills and competencies you have gathered over the years. Don't forget to include things you probably take for granted such as your computer literacy skills, languages, people skills etc. Some of these may seem a little less tangible than some of the more tangible skills such as numeracy and literacy, but they are nonetheless as important, so make sure you include them.

- **Personal Interests and Hobbies**

    Only include these if you have some interesting hobbies to include. Don't be tempted to make things up, as you can be sure it will come up at interview and you don't want to be embarrassed into admitting that you don't actually know that much about the subject. You won't leave a particularly good impression if this happens, and it could scupper what was otherwise a really good interview, so be warned.

    If you're not sure or your hobby is say, reading, give some examples of your reading material and be sure to include one or two business books, so that they can see that you're interested and committed. Mind you, if you do this, you will have to actually read the books you've listed, in case the interviewer has also read them and asks you about them. If you're really uncomfortable about this whole section, leave it out, but you're missing a trick if you do, as it gives the sifter and eventual interviewer a more rounded impression of who you are and what you're about.

- **References**

It is always desirable to provide references on your CV. Now let me provide a little more clarity here. What I mean by that is that it is good practice to include references if the length of your CV allows for it. If adding references will take you on to a third page, I would probably just include a statement such as: 'References are available on request.' Sifting processes won't usually be sifting on this criterion anyway. The important thing is that you have nominated referees. If you have the space however, do include them.

Now please allow me to provide a word of warning here. I know that your friends and family would probably wax lyrical about your fantastic qualities as a person, but that's not what a interviewer will be looking for. Please ensure your referees are able to vouch for you from the perspective of a professional and/or business capacity such as a previous boss, or a college or university tutor, or a professional person who knows you and can vouch for you in a reference. This is the same for anyone, no matter what job you are applying for i.e. a Road Sweeper or a Sales Director.

Unless you have a really open relationship with your current employer and have already notified them that you're looking for a different employer, and asked them to be a referee for you, then it's probably not a good idea to use them. You don't want to risk a letter arriving on the desk of your boss, who wasn't aware you were looking for alternative work. I've seen this happen too many times, hence my mention of it here.

If you are self employed and looking to get back in to employed work, it is acceptable to use employers you have had prior to being self employed, or failing this, you could perhaps use favoured clients who you have a good relationship with and are happy to provide you with a reference. Alternatively, perhaps an ex work colleague who would be happy to vouch for you.

Finally, you should always seek permission to use the person you nominate as a referee. It is common courtesy to let them know in advance that a reference may be sought and that you would like to use them for a reference.

General CV Structure and Format

The order that I have used above is the order you should use with your CV, so:

1. Your Personal Details
2. Personal Profile Statement (Your Hook)
3. Career experience
4. Education (Professional Education first, following by School/College education)
5. Skills and Competencies
6. Personal Interests and Hobbies
7. Referees

If you can keep your CV to two A4 sides that is the ideal as CV sifters say that more than this and they get bored and tend to miss whatever is written on the third page, so avoid this happening by trying to keep to 2 sides. Of course, if you have significant experience this is bound to take up more space and you will probably have no choice but to go on to a third page. So be it, but if this is the case, just make sure that all the impactful content you want to make an impression with, is contained within the first two sides, and leave the third side for the other less important stuff (referees; personal interests, hobbies, etc.)

Remember, your CV is effectively your shop window, your marketing material if you like, and you need to treat it as such. All good marketing material is tested to ensure it will do the job it is intended to do. So it is always good practice to let someone who is already in business, or better still, someone in HR, have a look over your CV to provide a constructive critique, particularly in the area of spelling and grammer. Did you spot the deliberate mistake? Well done if you did, irritating isn't it? Here is a book telling me how important spelling and grammar are, and they can't even get it right in their own material. I agree, and that's exactly what a CV sifter would be thinking, so please get your CV checked and double checked for these simple but destructive errors. We are less likely to spot our own mistakes, than we are someone else's. If you didn't spot the mistake, I think that just emphasises my point adequately!

Do I Use 'I' – My Name – or Passive Referral

Now what the hell does all that mean I can hear you asking? Well it is simply one of the areas people bother over quite regularly and they needn't. The question is: throughout my CV do I refer to myself as I as in 'I completed a technical competence project........' or use my name, such as: 'Jones completed a technical competence project........' or do you use a Passive reference such as: 'A technical competence project was completed......'. Well there are no hard and fast rules on this one, and any of the above styles are acceptable.

My personal preference would be to use the 'I' because that's what comes most naturally to me, and that's how I speak. The choice is really yours. All I would say is be consistent, always. If you start off using 'I' then make sure you stay with this all the way through, otherwise you will just irritate the sifter and you don't want to elicit any negative thoughts at this stage, because as we've already stated, this is your shop window, and people who want to sell their wares, don't put sub-standard goods in their shop window.

People who sift CVs do not have an infinite amount of time to do so - it will likely be only one of a myriad of tasks they have to complete day-to-day. Usually sifters will allocate an amount of time for each CV. This time will vary depending upon the person and the role being applied for. It is likely that more time will be spent sifting for a Chief Executive than for someone who is applying for a role as an Office Administrator. This is wrong you might say, well get over it, because it merely reflects reality. As long as they spend a relatively equal amount of time on all applicants for a particular role, that's the best you can hope for, and in any case, you'll never know.

Given this fact, and sometimes this time allocation will be as short as 30 seconds, you absolutely have to ensure your CV is as good as it can be. I have seen some horror stories in my time, and psychologically, there is a human tendency to 'switch off' from a CV that is badly written, or poorly structured. You're unlikely to be invited to interview and your content would have to be pretty amazing and compelling to convince a sifter to put you through for interview in these circumstances. You have been warned.

Embellishing, Exaggerating and Lying

It is an astounding statistic but recent studies have indicated that at least 25% of all CVs contain inaccurate data, due to embellishment, exaggeration and/or downright lying on the CV. **PLEASE, DO NOT DO THIS**. If you do you may scupper any chance of getting the job, and more importantly, if the inaccuracy is not detected at interview stage but comes to light later on when you have been in the job for a while, you could be sacked. How embarrassing would that be? So don't let it happen.

There is a very clear difference to constructing your CV so that it is presented in the very best light to a prospective employer, and lying or embellishing your CV. One is acceptable and the other isn't.

If you 'hand on heart' know that your CV contains only truthful facts, you will feel far more confident than if you go into an interview knowing that at any time, you might be asked a question about something you know to be a lie. Don't do this to yourself; it's embarrassing and humiliating to be shown up to be liar.

What we're talking about here is your honesty and integrity, and a prospective employer will not look favourably on someone who has shown themselves to be lacking in this very important quality. The question they would be asking themselves is: "Well if he/she can lie about that, what else could he/she be lying about?"

The Interview – Overview

OK, so you've successfully got through the sifting process and your invitation to an interview letter has landed on your door mat, now what do you do? Well you prepare – properly, that's what you do.

If you remember, we explained at the beginning of this report how to make sure your CV is tailored to the requirements of your prospective employer by asking them for a Role Profile. You could even go as far as asking them for a list of competencies that the role requires – they can only say no, if they don't feel you should have them.

Most businesses will be quite happy to let you have a Role Profile; after all you do need to know as much about the role you are applying for as possible.

So, let's assume you have now had the Role Profile emailed to you, what next? Well, you need to scrutinize this document to try and establish what competencies the role requires. You don't have to be exact here, you may not be able to precisely pinpoint the exact word, but you might be able to establish a sense of what the competency might be. For example: let's imagine that the role you have applied for is a Logistics Manager in a Transport Company and the Role Profile describes the need for accuracy and attention to detail. You can be absolutely sure that one of the competencies the company will be looking for is accuracy and attention to detail – they might call it something else as an overall word or phrase, but the meaning will be the same.

The process I advocate when I'm training this concept is to sit down with a high-lighter pen and high-light words or phrases that could be deemed to be a competency (or would indicate the need for a particular competency) as I read through the Role Profile.

Most businesses work with around 8 key competencies, so you need to see if you can pull at least 8 competencies out of the Role Profile. Competencies are broken down into two main categories: generic competencies and role specific competencies.

So by way of example, let's say we have the role of a Sales Person position, these might be:

Communication
(Articulate; expressive; positive body language; clarity of speech and written communications)

Administration
(Organisation; prioritising; processing; follow up; effective diary management and record keeping; database input management; self discipline)

Customer Friendly
(Friendly; Positive outlook; Personable; Presentable; Well groomed; Can-do attitude; Goes the extra mile; Attentive)

Selling Skills
(Sales process; negotiating; closing skills; rapport building; relationship management)

Prospecting and Customer Acquisition
(Telephone prospecting, database trawling, networking, postcode analysis, self marketing)

Product Knowledge
(Full range product knowledge, direct competitor product knowledge, funding and finance package knowledge)

> Numeracy and Accuracy
> (Mathematical adeptness; accurate recording of statistics; ability to calculate; attention to detail)

These are only a few to help understanding, but I'm sure you get the picture.

Now this is where it gets really interesting and where you can really make sure your preparation leaves no stone unturned. Let me explain:

The Interview Structure

Seasoned and trained interviewers usually work to an Interview Structure. What this means is a series of key competencies under which they have a number of competency based questions relative to that key competency.

For the sake of consistency, let's use the example of a Sales Person that we referred to above. A full list of Key Competencies might look something like the following:

1. Communication
2. Administration
3. Customer Orientation
4. Competition
5. Selling
6. Numeracy and Accuracy
7. Relationship Building
8. Persuasion
9. Negotiating
10. Team Working
11. Self Discipline

12. Self Development
13. Self Motivation

Now before you go into a complete spin, it's unlikely that there would be this many headings, as I've already stated most companies work to around 8, but I've included them to provide as many examples of Key Competencies for a Sales role as I can think of.

Now remember these are headings so beneath these headings will be the competency based questions. So once you've combed through the Role Profile and/or Job Description to try to identify the competencies, you can safely assume that these competencies will also form the headings in the interview structure,

Now that we've established what we believe the competencies are, and therefore what the headings are likely to be, we can now attempt to anticipate what questions might be asked for each competency (heading). Now before I provide you with examples, I need to tell you about what competency means and how this relates to 'competency based' interview questions.

Competency is a much misunderstood word and is often described as 'ability' or 'skill' neither of which is correct. There are many definitions, however, essentially competency is the consistent application of the accumulated skills, knowledge, behaviour and attitude an individual brings to their role. So in a nutshell, it is the action of 'doing' or 'applying' that renders someone competent.

Competency based questions are a method of questioning that seeks to establish what the applicant or candidate actually does in their current role, so the questions will be structured to establish this. The following are some basic competency based questions, just to give you an idea of the style of questions you are likely to be asked:

Selling:

- Tell me about a potential sale that you failed to close?
- Talk me through the sales process you follow from the moment a prospective customer enters your business?
- Give me an example of when the process didn't work for you?

Numeracy and Accuracy:

- On a scale of 1-10 how numerate are you?

- How does your Manager describe your accuracy? When did he/she last have to take you to task about this?
- When was the last paperwork error you made, and what was it?
- What were the implications of it? And how did you correct it?

Communication:

- Describe your communication style?
- What's good about it in your opinion?
- How do you strive to improve it?
- Tell me about a time when something you communicated was not received in the way you intended? How did you resolve it?

General Questions

- What are you accountable for in your current role?
- Tell me about a time when you took a risk at work?
- What was the outcome of taking that risk?
- When did you last disagree or challenge someone more senior to you at work?
- What was it about?
- What was the outcome?
- Talk me through a bad decision you have made in the past couple of years?

- How do you measure your success?

These are just a few examples to help your understanding of competency based questions.

Note that these questions are all specific and refer to an actual event that you may have encountered rather than a hypothetical event. That is because a hypothetical question will probably render a hypothetical answer. Let's take the first question above. It's asking you to tell the interviewer of a specific time that you failed to close a sale. If we take this question and ask it in a hypothetical way, it might go something like this:

"Tell me what you would do if you failed to close a sale."

There is a strong likelihood that the person being interviewed will answer this with a hypothetical answer such as:

"I would first make sure that I'd done everything possible to close the sale, and once I was happy that I had, I would make sure that the relationship I had with the customer was still in-tact even though they hadn't actu-

35

ally bought on the day, I could put them in my diary to follow up at some point in the future."

Not a bad answer you might be thinking, but is it really true? How would the interviewer know whether the person being interviewed would actually do that or not? It's far better to ask actual questions about actual activity (competency based), and to get real evidence of real action, rather than rely on information that may or may not be true, because there's no way of telling whether it is or it isn't. Too many people are skilled at giving text-book answers, and it's mainly when the interviewer is not skilled at asking competency based questions.

Where this is really powerful for someone applying for a job, is that although you don't know what questions you will be asked before you attend the interview, the fact that you've (hopefully) got them to send you the Role Profile, Job Description and/or the competencies of the role, you can then take an informed perspective of what questions you are most *likely* to be asked, and therefore can prepare your answers. Even if they don't ask the exact same questions as you anticipated, the fact that you have prepared a whole bunch of answers around competencies will allow you to answer the questions they *do* ask, far more competently and confidently, weaving in your prepared answers throughout the interview.

Even if the interviewer is not skilled at competency based questions, the fact that you've prepared a whole bunch of actual examples of how you've applied your skills, you will be head and shoulders ahead of everyone else that comes to the interview, and probably giving hypothetical answers all over the place.

So let's make this come alive for you. Let's say you have applied for the role of a Sales Person to sell photocopiers and you've asked for and been sent the Role Profile and/or the competencies for the role. You have gleaned from the Role Profile that sales process and closing skills are important for this role, along with 6 other competencies you believe you have identified. You can now begin to brainstorm all of the likely questions you might get around this subject. So for example, you believe the interviewer will ask a question around closing skills, or how you might have failed to close a deal. You should always think about questions that will demonstrate your application of a skill, and where you might have failed to apply the skill. These are the type of questions that competent interviewers ask. So you prepare an answer that goes something like this to the question: Tell me about a time you failed to close a deal?

"I usually use one of two preferred closing styles, namely the alternative close, or the assumptive close (*sales people will know what these are*). A couple of weeks ago, I found that a prospective client didn't react favourably to the assumptive close; I asked the customer who had not yet said they wanted to buy, when they would like to take delivery of their new photocopier? (*It could be any type of product, the principle of closing is the same*). They made it very clear they hadn't yet made the decision to buy. So I got us both a cup of coffee, leaving the prospective client to mull things over a little more.

When I returned with the coffee I said to the customer, "shall I give you some more time, or shall I get the order prepared now?" (giving an alternative) Again, the customer let me know that they weren't ready to buy yet. Having tried to ascertain what aspects they were still unsure of, so that I could help them, I still received a negative response. At this point, I backed off completely, and said "shall I just leave you to mull things over and you can come to me once you've made up your mind?" It was about 10 minutes later that the prospective client came over to my desk, apologising for the time they had taken, but also saying that on balance they were not quite ready to buy at that particular time, but that the figures were fine, it was just about business circumstances. We shook hands and I agreed to give them a call in two or three week's time. In fact before I had the chance to call, they called me, and wanted to proceed with the order.

Now the above answer tells the interviewer so many things about you. It demonstrates that you know about the various closing techniques, and that you understand that not all customers respond favourably to a 'close' technique. Also that although you failed to close the sale on the day, you were professional enough to keep the relationship with the customer intact, and that you adopted the skill of follow up calling to lost sales. So what you've effectively done here is turn a negative situation (where you failed to close a sale) into a positive by telling the interviewer how you managed yourself through this situation. No interviewer could fail to be impressed with an answer similar to that given above, because it demonstrates so many other great qualities of the person being interviewed.

Now what's great about this is that even if the interviewer asks a different question, you should be able to skilfully weave some of your 'practiced' information into your answer.

Yes, it does take a bit of time and preparation on your part, but if you want the job, surely a degree of investment in time has got to be worth your while.

I absolutely guarantee that once you go through this process you will significantly increase your chances of getting short-listed for final interview, where you will use the exact same principles to prepare for that.

I have used this technique myself to land a number of key jobs that I have wanted in the past. It has worked for me every time. Also for the hundreds of people I have trained over the years in these very same techniques.

The bi-product of preparing in this way is that you also come across in interviews as thorough; credible; professional; prepared; and believable. You will make so much more impact than if you go in cold and unprepared.

So just to recap on the process so far:

- Phone company for Role Profile and / or Job Description and see if they will also provide you with the competencies for the role. If you don't ask, they can't say 'yes' can they.

- If they don't provide the competencies but do provide the documents, which most companies

> will be happy to do, read through them several times identifying the key competencies that most definitely will be described within them. This will be easier than you think.
>
> - Once you think you have identified as many of the key competencies as you can, you can start considering what types of questions might be asked around each key competency.
>
> - Now that you have a good idea of the type of questions that might be asked, you can now think about how you can answer those questions, always putting yourself in as positive a light as possible. My sample questions a little later on will help you here.

The next section deals with more of those difficult and sometimes killer questions. If you prepare well and heed the techniques in this report, you will improve your chances of getting the job you want significantly.

6

Those Killer Interview Questions and How to Answer Them

What follows are many of those very difficult questions that can sometimes floor a candidate and render them a crumbling wreck in the eyes of the interviewer. Most competent interviewers ask these types of questions to assess how well you think on your feet, and sometimes to determine how honest you are prepared to be, so you might as well accept it and just make sure you are as well prepared for them as you can be.

The following is not an exhaustive list, but enough for you to get the gist of how to answer these types of questions when you encounter them.

Is this cheating I hear you say? Well in my opinion "No I don't believe it is." It's just making sure you are as prepared as you can be for the situation you are in. As a past employer of many hundreds of people, it is such a joy to interview someone who has clearly prepared well for the interview. It is evident that they have researched the company well and know about the key areas of the business, its purpose, its values, and any other relevant and pertinent information. They are also able to adequately answer competency based questions and don't get flustered when you throw in a difficult or negatively biased question. They eloquently manoeuvre their way through these questions and maintain their credibility and composure throughout.

Yes of course it is blatantly obvious they have prepared, rehearsed and practiced their answers, but in my view that just tells me that this person is thorough and professional and wants the job enough to go to so much trouble.

Don't get me wrong they have to able to back it up when they're in the role, otherwise their employment will be short-lived, but I've never had someone who has performed really well at interview that hasn't made the grade once they joined the business.

Before we embark on the Killer Questions, there are likely to be questions around your redundancy, so let's get these out of the way first. These types of questions will vary but I have given a number of examples that hopefully you'll find useful:

I Note You Left Your Previous Job Almost Four Months Ago?

Any Interviewer will pick up on gaps in your CV or application form, so it is perfectly reasonable to ask this question. The best policy is to be honest and succinct in answering this. Of course the Interviewer may want to probe a little further, and I've provided some sample answers later on for when this happens. In the meantime, answers like the following would be fine:

"Yes, the company I worked for were struggling financially and needed to off-load about 25% of the workforce. I was made redundant in September this year. It was a bit of a shock at first, but I've taken a breathing space, and some time for myself and I'm really excited about what the future holds for me now."

"Yes that's right I was made redundant in September. I've taken the opportunity to brush up on my ....xyz... skills doing a fast-track course in.....xyz... with the local college which I think will really help me in the field of jobs I'm applying for."

"Yes I was made redundant in September. I've been doing various interim roles on a fixed term contract basis in the meantime, which has really helped prepare me for my next full-time position, it's been invaluable."

A word of warning, you will in all probability be probed on the types of company and roles you have been working, so be prepared.

The next question is a variation on the theme, but subtly different in that it requires a little more detail in your answer:

Have You Found Coping With Redundancy Difficult?

This is a subtly clever question, and the Interviewer may have a number of reasons for asking it, such as trying to determine your state of mind (we talked about this earlier), or perhaps trying to establish if you've been turned down by lots of other companies, or even your drive and determination levels. There could be a myriad of reasons, so all the more reasons to make sure you answer it as polished and professional as possible. So let's have a look at a number of ways you could answer this question:

>   1. *"Well it was a bit of a shock when the redundancy happened and I did need some time to get my head around the prospect of what it meant. Never having been in this situation before, it was a completely new experience. After speaking with my wife (or husband), I decided that I*

should take some time to retrench and take stock. There had been a few things that I'd always promised myself I'd do and never had the time to do them, such as ....(whatever you have a personal interest in) which has been great and I'm immensely grateful that I've had the opportunity to do it. I also took the time to really consider the type of company I wanted to work for, and promised myself that I wouldn't just accept the first job that came along. It's also been a number of years since I've been in the job market, so I've also spent some time dusting down my CV and updating it."

2. *"In my previous job, one thing that I wished I'd been better at was....(computer skills; or presentation skills; or coaching skills...or any skill that you have actually learned since you left your previous job), so I decided to invest some time and money in learning this new skill. I'm so pleased I did because I feel so much more confident now that I have more to offer a prospective employer."*

3. *"My redundancy came at a time when my (wife; husband; mother; father etc) had some important issues that required my support. Given my circumstances it made practical sense for me to provide the support for the few weeks (months)*

> *it took to resolve. I am now 100% focused on my future and my search for the right job with the right company."*

4. *"As difficult as redundancy is, I'm very pragmatic and philosophical about these things. I try to see my situation as simply a commercial decision that needed to be taken in order for my previous company to survive the current economic climate. It isn't personal it's just an inevitable consequence of such a significant downturn in trading conditions. I'm quite an upbeat and positive person, so I try to look at these situations as an opportunity."*

The above four example answers would be considered by any interviewer to be good answers. None of them would create concern in the Interviewers' mind about you, and in fact the question is a fantastic opportunity for you to communicate that your head and heart are in the right place (metaphorically speaking of course).

Please don't be tempted to share any frustrations, irritations and bitterness about your redundancy with your Interviewer. They might on the surface seem empathetic, but trust me you will be creating serious doubt in their mind about your suitability. If you harbour these feelings keep them to yourself; you won't do yourself any favours by sharing your doom and gloom. No-one likes to be around people who whinge, moan and gripe, least of all a prospective employer.

Also, if you are taking your previous employer to a tribunal, or are yet to settle the financial details of your package, or worse still you are in dispute with them, DO NOT mention it unless it is brought up by the Interviewer. In this case, be as general and as vague as possible, so something like:

"We've just finalised the details of my redundancy package, so I can now focus 100% on my search for the right job."

Or

"I'd never been in that situation before so I thought it best get some advice, and everything got resolved amicably which is great."

Or if they come right out and ask you if you've ever taken a previous employer to a tribunal, you will have no choice but to answer the question honestly. There's no point lying as you will only get found out in the end, so in this circumstance something like the following will suffice:

"Yes I have, and because it was all new to me I felt I needed to take legal advice, and I'm pleased to say it was resolved quickly and without bad feeling on either side."

Most prospective employers feel uneasy and uncomfortable if someone has taken a previous employer to a tribunal. They'll never tell you that, but it is a fact. The best you can do is hope that the question doesn't come up, but be prepared just in case it does.

OK, let's get going on these Killer Questions.

What Do You Know About Our Company?

Well there's absolutely no excuse for not being able to answer this one. If you're applying for a job with any company PLEASE find out as much about them as you can BEFORE you attend for interview.

These days we have the internet at our disposal and the vast majority of your research can be done here visiting their website, where you should be able to pick up quite a lot of key information.

Alternatively, you can send for brochures or visit the company personally to pick up material, and possibly speak with receptionists who are often quite talkative and helpful especially if they are bored. You can be honest and tell them you're attending an interview and want to know more about the company in readiness for your interview.

Who Would You Say Are Our Main Competitors and Why?

Again, this should be relatively easy. Look at their website and ascertain their main business, then look at the websites of companies selling the same or similar products or services. Do comparisons against businesses which are similar in size and profile. There is a good chance that these are likely to be main competitors. Even if you get this one wrong, the fact that you've done your research will go a long way, and will let the interviewer know you've prepared.

If You Were Appointed MD of Our Business Tomorrow What Changes Would You Make?

This one is only likely to be asked to Managers and above. If that's you, be careful on this, as you don't want to come across as critical of the business before you've even started. An answer similar to the following would probably do the trick in most cases:

"If I were appointed tomorrow, I probably wouldn't change anything immediately. I'd first of all want to know an awful lot more about the business than I currently know, such as which parts of the business are successful and why, and which parts are not successful and why. Also, who are my strong Leaders and who are not so strong and is there a correlation between the two aspects. So in summary, I'd take a period of time to assess the business before coming up with a change strategy, and only then if it was required as Change for Change sake is never a good idea – I'd only want to fix what was broken."

What Are Your Weaknesses? (Usually asked after What Are Your Strengths)

Again, some thought needs to be applied here, as you don't want to air your dirty linen in public and certainly not at an interview. You don't need to lie you just need to be a little canny about how you answer the question. The key here is to turn your answer around, so that you answer the question but at the same time turn the weakness into a potential strength. Here's how I answer this question when asked:

"I sometimes get really impatient with myself. If I'm not achieving the results I want in the time that I've given myself to achieve them, I get quite frustrated and then put myself under unnecessary pressures to get to my goal. This has often resulted in me working well into the night to get something done. However, I now try to avoid this happening by being very organised and self-disciplined when setting myself goals and objectives."

What you've skilfully done here is answer the question (honestly I hope) but also turned a negative into a positive and once again told the interviewer an awful lot about your character as a person.

What Would Your Boss Say Are Your Main Strengths and Weaknesses?

This is a variation on the Strengths/Weakness question, but is often asked. Following are a couple of answers that I have personally used in the past:

"With regard to my Main strength, I believe he would say that I always go the extra mile; give far more to any task or project than most, and that he can leave me alone to get on with it, which frees him up to work with others that perhaps need his attention and help more, I know he appreciates this because he has told me so often. I know and passionately believe that hard work and putting your all in to a job, is the quickest way to get on in any business, and it's also so much more enjoyable."

In relation to my main weakness, when I first started in the job I used to get irritated with myself and impatient if I didn't get things done perfectly, and in the shortest of time. After a couple of feedback sessions with my boss, I learned that perfection wasn't necessary, but that high standards were. He taught me that always striving for perfection is a weakness not strength; mainly because it takes so much time and in the main is not attainable. This was a fantastic learning curve for me, and the opposite of what I'd always believed previously. Since then I've always achieved very high standards, but if something I do is fantastic but not perfect I'm fine with that, and of course because I'm not spending time striving for perfection, I get loads more done.

What Sets You Apart from Other Candidates We May Be Interviewing For This Role?

Now you can't just say, well I don't know the other candidates, so I can't comment. Well you could but may I respectfully suggest you don't as it will go down like a lead balloon. This is what is called a Shop Window Question, so you need to prepare a Shop Window Answer. This is your opportunity to sell yourself to the interviewer. Someone once answered this question to me (as the interviewer) in the following way (not necessarily the same words, but the same key message):

"With every Company I've worked for over the past 13 years, I've been promoted several times to the point of going as far as I can go in that company, and usually only left because there was no further I could have gone there. Many of my current friends are ex bosses that I've worked for. Loyalty is an extremely important quality to me, and I've found throughout my career that when you are loyal to someone, they repay that loyalty in return. Because I always like to progress in the companies I work for, I always make a point of supporting my Manager in whatever way I can, taking on extra work, working extra hours, doing the things that everyone else avoids, - I really enjoy a challenge and love to be stretched, as that's the way I learn best. A number of my previous Managers have often said they wished they'd had 10 of me on their team, so I know

from experience that I really am set apart from the majority, although of course I cannot comment about the other candidates as I don't know them."

Well let me tell you, this person blew me away with this answer. He answered with passion and with absolute clarity. He looked me straight in the eye when he said those words, and I had no doubt that he meant every one of them. He got the job and performed and behaved in exactly the way he described. He is indeed a very good friend today, and I know he's tickled pink about me using this answer in this book.

Why Should We Consider You For This Role?

This is really a variation on the above theme so again, an answer similar to that above would be great. Please don't be tempted to say something like: *"Because I'm just the best there is, I'm fantastic at what I do."* That may be true, but it's not giving the interviewer any specific qualities that they can assess you by. Prepare some specific qualities that you can weave in to this answer that will leave the interviewer impressed and wanting to know more about you. Although difficult, these questions are great questions to get at interview because they provide you with a readymade platform to 'sell yourself.' This is not the time to be overly reserved or to hide your light under a bushel!

"When I first read the role profile and job description, I got really excited. It just all felt so right for me, in fact it felt as if the job had been written for me." then continue as in above answer...

Who Is the Worst Boss You Have Ever Worked For and Why?

The interviewer won't be looking for a name here, just a description of your worst boss. You can be honest but just be careful how you answer – you should choose your words wisely, not being overly critical and personal, but more evaluative rather than judgemental. This question assesses where your tolerance levels are in the way that you are managed and can reveal a lot about a candidate in the way that they answer. Consider the following two contrasting answers:

Example No. 1

"The worst boss I ever had was a few years ago when I worked in the XYZ industry. Actually he was a really nice guy, but had never received any management training, so consequently often didn't manage his reactions and responses particularly well. This sometimes resulted in him losing his temper and flying off the handle at someone in front of their colleagues. It happened to me once and I can remember feeling really embarrassed. I'd made a small mistake and told him immediately. Even though I'd already corrected the

mistake he still balled me out in front of everyone. It was a real shame because other than his short temper, he had the potential to be a good manager."

Example No. 2

"The worst boss I ever had was someone that when I think of him now makes me really angry. He was awful and picked on people including me for no reason. He expected blood out of a stone, and nothing I or anyone else ever did was good enough. In the end I just did enough not to get criticised, and one day I told him exactly what I thought of him, before telling him where he could put his job. I left that very same day."

I hope it is evident to you which of the above answers is the better and more appropriate of the two. The first is evaluative and balanced (he's a really nice guy; he had the potential to be a good manager) and sticks to the facts without displaying emotion. The second is emotive and negatively charged and leaves the interviewer wondering how much of the Managers reactions were justified. It also tells them that you are prone to bursts of unpredictability and negative reaction (I told him where he could put his job; I left the very same day). This second answer would raise some very serious questions in the interviewers mind about you, no matter how justified and honest your answer was.

What Other Businesses Have You Applied To, and How Far Are You In That Process?

Again you should be honest here, but let the interviewer know that although you have applied for say two other posts with other companies, your preference is this company and in fact would be prepared to put the other two on hold if you felt that there was a reasonable chance that you might have an opportunity to join them. This will send a clear message that they are your preference and will reassure them that you are not just throwing your hat in the ring to see which ones result in an offer and you'll decide then.

Yes it's playing politics a wee bit, but sometimes you just have to do what you have to do. Dishonest, maybe, just a little bit, but if you told the interviewer that you'd be happy to join whichever of the three companies were to make you an offer, you'd probably scupper your chances. So needs must on occasions I'm afraid.

What's The One Question You Dread Being Asked At Interview?

This can be a really difficult question to answer. But it needn't be. Let me offer some wise words that might help here. You could be clever and say, *"This one."* But that wouldn't impress the interviewer much. So you could say one of the following:

"The question you asked about my weaknesses, it's never great to admit you've got them, but we all have, so I can understand why you ask it."

or

"The worst boss question, because it's never good to think about people in that way."

You get the point. Choose a difficult question that's already been asked. Hopefully you will have answered it well, so there should be no problem citing it here. If you've really prepared well you could use a different example and one that hasn't been asked yet (but you will need to have prepared a really good answer), but do so in the full knowledge that you will be expected to answer it at that point too, because the question following it will be "Why do you dread being asked that question?"

How Do You Prefer To Be Managed and Why?

This is quite a revealing question as it gives so much away about how you like to work. If you say you like a lot of direction say it in a way that communicates to the interviewer why this is so, for example:

"I like a lot of direction from a Manager because I like to know exactly what's expected of me so that I can do

my very best to ensure I achieve the very high standards I set for myself."

If you don't provide the *'so that I can..........'* element, the interviewer could think that you lack confidence or ability to work under your own steam, so always qualify what you say with a positive. Alternatively, you could answer with the following:

"I like to work under my own steam mainly. I'm really happy to receive direction from my Manager but then I like to be left to get on with it. I pride myself on having very high standards and have always had really good relationships with my Managers. I think that's because they've known they can rely on me to get on with the task in hand, and that if I need support or direction I will come to them for this."

This answer instils a degree of confidence in the interviewer that you are someone who can be left to get on with the job, and won't require a 'high maintenance' approach from a manager. Be honest with this question, but don't forget to add in the qualifying bit, *"so that I can..."* in order not to give the wrong impression.

Tell Me About The Last Time You Got Annoyed At Work?

Again, the interviewer is looking for how you react to annoyance and irritation, so do choose and prepare what you are going to say carefully. Most people get annoyed or irritated sometimes, so it wouldn't be believable to say *"I never get annoyed – ever."* If it's true and you say it, that might create an impression of being too laid back and not passionate or caring enough. Better to say something along the lines of:

"It happened a few months ago now (so not a frequent occurrence) a colleague had asked me for some support in putting a presentation together that they had been asked to present the following morning, as they were stacked out with work and would have really struggled getting it done. I did the work at home in my own time, and even sacrificed going to see my son play football that evening. Once it was complete at around 11.00pm I emailed the presentation to my colleague so that they could get familiar with the content and make any changes prior to the meeting the next morning. Within a few minutes of sending it, I received an email back telling me that the meeting the following morning had been postponed until the following week. My colleague even told me that they'd received the notification of postponement at 7.15 that evening, but they'd forgotten to let me know.

Well yes I have to admit I wasn't best pleased, so decided not to respond to the email and just to sleep on it to calm down. I did speak to my colleague about how their thoughtlessness had made me feel and they were very remorseful. It was just a case of them not thinking, so we both decided to forget about it and move on. I'm not someone who sulks or bears grudges, and I do value the working relationship I have with this person, so yes I was annoyed but I quickly got over it, as I know it wasn't my colleague's intent to cause me unnecessary work."

What Are the Positive Things Your Work Colleagues Say About You?

This might feel a little bit uncomfortable as you're being asked to say good things about yourself, even though they are things that others would say about you. Well you will just have to accept that the question has been asked and so you need to answer it. It's OK to show a degree of shyness or humility here, the interviewer will know how difficult this is. Nonetheless you will still need to answer. Don't go over the top, but keep your answer balanced. Consider the following:

"My work colleagues tell me that I'm hard working and ambitious. They have also said that I am determined and focused particularly when there is a goal or

deadline to achieve. I also know that they value my input because they ask for it frequently. I'm also the one that they tend to turn to if they are struggling or have made a mistake. I would always help a colleague in need if it was within my power to do so."

The above answer is not too gushing, but balanced and just right.

What Are the Negative Things Your Work Colleagues Say About You?

This one might feel uncomfortable for a different reason. If you don't have any negative examples for this, just say so, if you do, just remember to temper how your word them. For example don't say:

"Well my colleagues tell me that I'm too laid back." This won't impress at all. Far better to choose something that won't impact on the interviewer at all, such as:

"My colleagues tell me that I can be too focused on achieving my goals sometimes, and that I need to slow down a little. I can see why they would say that, but it's who I am I can't relax if I have stuff outstanding that needs to be done."

I trust you get my point here. It's merely turning the negative around to a positive. Remember what we said earlier, we don't want to focus on any negatives if at all possible. After all, being at an interview is like being in your own shop window.

What Have You Told Your Employer About Where You Are Today?

This one is checking your integrity, so be careful how you answer. Don't say *"I've put in enough time over the years, so I figure they owe me, so I've said I've got a doctors' appointment."* A far better answer would be:

"I'm working my lunch hour today to make up for it. I told my employer that I had some personal business to attend to which they were fine with."

This demonstrates honesty and integrity.

"I booked a half day holiday from my annual leave to be here."

This demonstrates commitment.

By the way, it helps if either of the above two examples are the truth!

Tell Me About A Time When You Didn't Get On With One or More Team Members?

It is perfectly acceptable to say that you've always found that you've enjoyed good working relationships with your work colleagues, and you can't recall a time when you didn't – that's fine, but the interviewer may not be entirely convinced. Alternatively, if you have a strong enough answer, you could use that. What I mean by a strong enough answer is something like the following:

"There was a time a few years ago when I joined XYZ company and I was the new person in an established team. I encountered some resistance and even animosity from two of the other members of the team, and I didn't understand why. I eventually discovered that the person who had been my predecessor had been sacked for stealing from the company, but was best friends to these two people. I felt that they resented my presence in the team and made things quite difficult for me for a few months. It was a difficult situation but I'm quite resilient and dislike bad feeling immensely, so within a few weeks I was beginning to add value and show my worth to the team by helping and supporting them whenever I had the opportunity to do so, things like

staying late to help them out, taking on some of their tasks, even to the two difficult people too, and this had a really positive effect on the others in the team. It took a few months to win over the two resistant people, but I got there eventually and went on to have a really good working relationship with all of them."

This is just an example, but it's a good answer on a number of levels because it demonstrates your positive traits such as willingness to do over and above what is required, and to help your colleagues when in need, and your ability to engender a positive team working environment. The first answer is ok, but the second answer is powerful.

What Is Your Most Significant Achievements In Your Current Role?

This is another great question, but one that you definitely need to think about and prepare for.

It's no good answering with some fluffy wishy-washy answer that the interviewer will not perceive as 'significant.' If the most significant thing you can think of is that you got a 'thank you and well done' email from your boss, they could think that good work from you is not a frequent occurrence. The following is a much better answer: (but remember it has to be true, don't make stuff up, you'll be sussed very quickly).

"I have been awarded employee of the month three times this year so far, and last year I won the 'Employee of the Year' award for the whole company."

Now you could just leave it there, but expand on this even further, tell the interviewer what is it about what you do, and how you do it that has led to your continued success in this area, so something like:

"Our Managing Director sent out a newsletter in which he described my contribution to the company as 'invaluable and inspiring.' He also said that I was one of the most positive people in the company and that I was a role model to the younger and newer people in the business."

So although you've told the interviewer of your achievement you've also given them so much more information about you, and not in a big-headed or self righteous way, but in the third person (quoting your MD) which is a fabulous technique to use. To think about and prepare for this answer, consider all areas of your role:

- Have you introduced an idea or suggestion that has been implemented and made a significant difference to the working practices of the department or business?

- Have you supported a different area of the business without asking for or expecting reward or payment and what impact did it have.

- Have you helped younger less experienced members of the team to get on in their role without being asked to do so, has it been recognised and what was the impact on the those people? And is it something you continue to do as a matter of course?

- Do customers frequently write letters to the company about the great service you afford them, and don't forget to tell the Interviewer what exactly the customers say about you (remember: third person).

- Have you been asked to represent the company at an event? Again, don't forget to say why you were chosen, and what impact you had at the event (positive of course).

If you really can't think of anything significant that you've done, then you'll have to answer it as best you can, but my challenge to you is to ask yourself why? Are you really living your life (including your working life) in the best way you can. I would suggest not, so think about it and consider if this fact had a bearing on you being chosen for redundancy? I know this is a difficult thing to have to admit, but businesses won't off-load great people before they've off-loaded the mediocre people, and if you don't add value or contribute anything of significance, then you have to be honest with yourself.

Talk Me Through The Last Time You Went the Extra Mile?

Now be careful with this one, as this is a question I personally ask when I'm interviewing and you'd be surprised how many people answer it by telling you about something that is part of their role anyway. So referring to an answer that was given to me by someone I interviewed for a Sales Person's position, he told me this:

"It was a couple of days ago actually. I had a customer who I'd sold a car to about two years ago, and every three months I make a point of giving my custom-

ers a courtesy call to see how things are with the car and basically keep the relationship in-tact for when they are ready to change their car. Anyway, I made the call and it was evident that the customer was in a bit of a state. He is an elderly gentleman and normally we have a little chat, but this time he seemed really agitated and distracted. I apologised for the imposition and said it was obviously not a good time to call. He told me that he wasn't feeling too well and didn't feel able to drive, but that he needed his prescription from the Chemist fairly urgently. He'd thought about trying to walk there but it was a couple of miles away and again he didn't think he'd be able to make it there and back. So I got in the car, went to his home, picked up the prescription and went off to the chemist to get it, and then returned it to him. Whilst at the chemist, they knew the gentleman and had told him that they did provide a service to deliver prescriptions, but that so far he had declined any help. I took the pamphlets with me and gave them to the gentleman with his prescription. Obviously a very proud man, he looked embarrassed and grateful at the same time. The gentleman called me this morning to thank me again, and then called my boss to tell him also. Now it was my turn to be embarrassed."

Now I had no way of knowing whether what this guy told me was the truth or not, but either he was a great liar, because the story just rolled off his tongue, or he was indeed telling the truth.

However, he did get the job and about six or seven months later, he had just taken an order for a new car, and the customer had asked to be introduced to the General Manager – me. He introduced this elderly gentleman to me, and I must admit it didn't click at first, until he started to recount a story of how this sales person had helped him when he was in urgent need and that for the rest of his life he would never buy a car from anyone else, and had referred many of his friends to this lad also.

There had in fact been many other instances of this sales person going the extra mile and within a year he was one of the most successful sales people I'd ever had working for me. He now owns his own successful car sales business (funny that isn't it). We're still in touch to this day, and I have his permission to share this story.

So the learning here is try to think of something that really is going the extra mile, not just something that you should do as part of your role anyway. If you can't think of anything, well maybe you should ask yourself the question – Why?

On A Scale of 1-10 Where Are You In Relation to How Much Value You Add In Your Current Role?

Now this is a really tricky question so be careful how you answer it, because the question that will follow it is: So what would you need to do to get you to a 10?

So let's suppose you say 7 or 8, the interviewer will then ask you, what you would need to do to get to a 10, and then you're stumped unless you've prepared. So again let's assume you've said 8, and the interviewer has asked the second question, something like the following might be a useful answer:

"If I'd put myself at 10, I would be saying that there is nothing else I could do to add even more value to what I do, I'd be perfect, and I don't believe that is ever the case. However, I'd probably say that I need to take even more tasks off my boss to free up some of his time to do some higher level projects that I know he's keen to get involved in. The only reason I haven't so far is that I'm currently learning some of these things and therefore not quite ready to take them off him yet, but I'm not too far off being ready, but even then I wouldn't put myself at a 10 because I'll always think there is more I can do, it's just the way I am."

Bear in mind that the interviewer is likely to ask you what things you are currently learning, so you need to be able to answer. Also expect the interviewer to also question why you want to leave if you are in a process of development.

This is a good answer. The interviewer is asking it to uncover any development areas that exist, and although you will have these – we all do, you don't want to air them at an interview. Time enough once you've got the job to focus on development areas. This answer focuses on your belief that you can never get to a 10 because of your belief that there is always something we can do to improve. It also communicates how willing you are to take on extra responsibility from your boss, and also about your sense of self-discipline.

Do You Have Personal and Business (or career) Goals For Yourself and If So, What Are They?

Again, if you haven't got any goals now's the time to decide on some, write them down, and be versed in them for if and when this question is asked. There's no point giving example answers here, as these are personal to each individual. However, I'm happy to share my own with you for this year:

1. To earn 100% more income than I did last year.

2. To complete and publish the two books I am currently in the process of writing by March this year.

3. To expand my seminar business to operate outside of the West Midlands by May this year.

4. To launch my Information Publishing business by June this year.

5. To expand my Professional Speaking business from one engagement per month to three engagements per month by June this year.

Note all of my goals are specific. They say exactly what I propose to achieve and by when. This makes them far more meaningful to me, and it also means that I can benchmark myself against these at any point to see how much progress I'm making towards them. In terms of goal setting, we need to make sure that they are S.M.A.R.T. It stands for the following:

S -   Specific

M -   Measureable

A -   Achievable but Stretching

R -   Realistic

T -   Time bound

So in setting my goals I have made sure that they do indeed comply with the above. All of them are measurable, and I have considered feasibility in terms of what I think is both Realistic and Achievable, but also stretching. There would be little point in setting a goal that is so far above what is achievable, that I end up not achieving it. Yes I know that many other experts advocate aiming for the moon, so that you'll get to the stars, and I also subscribe to this school of thinking, but for my goals, I keep them just in reach and have never failed to achieve them so far – so it works for me.

A client that I am currently coaching and mentoring has the following goals:

1. To obtain promotion to the position of Operations Director by September this year.

2. To be earning a salary of £100,000 by end of this year.

3. To complete his MBA within 3 years from now.

4. To take his wife on a second honeymoon to Venice in June this year.

5. To be completely computer literate in Powerpoint and Excel by end of April this year.

(Computers and IT are currently a major weakness and development area for him).

A friend's son who I coached a few weeks ago, has the following goals:

1. To get a job within the next two months.

2. To enrol at college or night school to learn a trade (electrician) September this year.

3. To have his own (or rented) flat by end of this year.

4. To be earning at least £20,000 pa by end of this year.

5. To start a part time e-bay business selling memorabilia (which is his passion) by May this year.

The reason I'm sharing these with you is to demonstrate how diverse and different they all are. Goals are personal, and only mean something to the person who they belong to. However, there is another reason for having them, particularly if you are job searching and that is because it's a questions that is often asked at Interview, and trust me there is no worse answer to the question "Do You have any personal or business goals, and if so what are they?" than to simply hear "No I don't." Interviewers ask this question to gauge ambition and drive and a "No I don't" answer definitely won't give the right impression.

Where Do You See Yourself In Five Years Time?

Again quite a common question at Interview and it's usually asked to assess ambition and drive. Saying something like: *"I'd like your job when you move up in your career"* is fine if not a little smug. However, saying *"I'd like to be your boss by then"* definitely won't win you any brownie points in the interview stakes and neither would: *"I think I'll probably be the same position as I am now if I get this job."* I hope you can see why, without any explanation. Far better to shape your answer to something like the following:

"I'm quite ambitious but also realistic, so I'd like to think that by then I would have progressed in the organisation to say a couple of promotions and enjoying a greater level of responsibility. I'm loyal and I learn quickly so would look to constantly be working on my personal development, some of which I'm sure could benefit you as my boss as I am able to be delegated to which would free up your time to do other higher level work."

If You Were An Animal Which One Would It Be and Why?

Now this is not the type of question any self-respecting and professional interviewer will ask you, but it is one that occasionally gets asked by people who can't think of anything else to ask, so you might as well prepare for it.

All I will say here, is choose your animal carefully. Choose an animal that reflects all your positive traits. So saying a fox (cunning), or rat (vermin), wouldn't be a good idea. Think of the characteristics of different kinds of animals and decide which one suits your style for example a cat. Your answer might go something like this:

"I would say a cat, as cats are both loyal and independent and they are also self sufficient but enjoy the company of other species such as humans, other cats and sometimes even dogs. They are intelligent and resourceful and are happy to fend for themselves when the need arises."

You can see that this would be considered a good answer, even by an inexperienced interviewer.

What Do I Do If I Don't Understand a Question?

Well the worst thing you can do is try to answer the question without really understanding it - This will likely result in you sounding unsure or not answering it confidently or worse still giving a rambling or 'round the houses' answer. Far better to be honest and say something like:

"I'm sorry I don't think I understand the question, could you expand a little on it for me?

or

"I'm sorry, do you mean.........x y z ....or have I misunderstood the question?"

Most interviewers will appreciate your honesty and will re-phrase the question to help your understanding.

Questions That You Shouldn't Be Asked at Interview

(Because of their Inappropriate and/or Unethical Nature)

Now I am going provide some examples here of the type of questions which may be deemed to be inappropriate / unethical, and in some cases even illegal, if they are asked at interview.

The law protects us from discrimination on the grounds of race, religion, disability, trade union membership, age, marital status, and sex. So you can see the discrimination grounds are quite extensive. You will need to make a judgement call as to whether you believe the interviewer is being deliberately discriminatory, or they are just poor interviewers with a lack of knowledge. You may decide just to answer the question as best you can and move on to the next question, it's your call.

In my opinion, there's never an excuse for discriminatory questions, but sometimes inexperienced interviewers clumsily ask such questions with no ill-intent. This is still no defence in the eyes of the law, and if taken to a tribunal the company would be required to demonstrate from their records that they had made their decision fairly. Employers are required to 'select' the right person for the job, and not to make their recruitment decisions on the basis of information gathered that may be of a discriminatory nature.

So vast and complex is this subject that suffice to say I am not going in to any great detail here, but just to warn you that occasionally inexperienced interviewers will ask clumsy discriminatory questions, and occasionally you will also trip over deliberate discriminatory questions. You will have to make a judgement call as to how to deal with it. You may decide to note the question and then get some legal advice. This is of course your right but be aware that it will be very time-consuming, although if you believe it to be deliberate, it may well be worth pursuing, but do take advice first.

So let's look at just a few examples of these inappropriate, unethical and possibly illegal type questions:

1. **Do you have children (or are you intending to have children)?**

    This in most cases would be considered to be discriminatory. It is likely that this question would be asked of a female and not of a male.

This type of question is often asked to check on the likelihood of the company having to pay maternity pay in the future, or whether there could be any gaps in employment. It is not a fair basis to make a selection decision.

2. **How do you think your age might hamper your ability to do this job?**

   Again, this is likely to be discriminatory on the grounds of age, and would not be asked to someone who was perhaps younger. Therefore it is clearly indicating that the selection decision is being influenced by the age of the person and not entirely on whether they are the best person for that job.

3. **Where Were You Born?**

   This could be deemed to be indirect discrimination, as it is irrelevant to whether you are the best person for the job.

4. **Have You Got a Partner or Boyfriend (or Girlfriend)?**

Again, in most cases this is irrelevant and should not form part of the selection process, and may be deemed to be discriminatory.

5. How Important Is Belonging to a Trade Union to You?

This has no relevance on whether someone is the best person for the job and should not be used as part of the selection process.

6. What Religion Are You?

Once again we need to ask ourselves what relevance this has to selecting the best person for the job, and clearly it doesn't.

7. If We Employed You, You'd be The Only Black Member of An All-White Team, How Do Think You'd Get On In This Situation?

It is clear with this question that the interviewer is considering the race position here and this is likely to be deemed to be discriminatory.

You will note that I've not included a question on disability, and that is because this is a complex area of law. Employers cannot discriminate against anyone with disabilities, and are obliged to adjust their recruitment and selection processes in order to accommodate disabled people. Examples include access to interview rooms, and special arrangement to allow disabled people to be able to take tests that may require adjustment of the testing processes, facilities, approaches to testing and so on). The law considers what is reasonable for an employer in these cases.

I would urge anyone who is disabled to gain specialist advice on this complex subject if you feel that you have been discriminated against.

There are many variations on the theme of these inappropriate/unethical/illegal type questions, but for ease of understanding a company's selection process must be based upon 'the best person for the job' and not on irrelevant areas that the law provides protection in.

Please note that it is perfectly legal and normal for companies to gather such information as age, gender, marital status, and health on application forms. This is fine as long as the information is not used as part of their selection process.

If you are unsure whether an interview you have attended was lawful or not on any of the grounds listed above, and you want further clarification, in the first instance I would recommend your local Citizen's Advice Bureau, who will be happy to advise and point you in the right direction.

8

Creating Impact

Be aware that according to research, we form 90% of our opinion of others within the first 90 seconds of meeting them. At an interview you will want to make the very best impression you can.

Try to control your nerves, there is nothing worse than shaking someone's very hot and sweaty hands – please, I'm not being unkind but you must try to relax and to give the very best impression you can. I will share with you some techniques and tips for achieving this right now.

When we communicate face-to-face (as in an interview) there are 3 communication methods in use, namely:

- Body-language which accounts for 57% of the communication
- The words that we use which accounts for 7% of the communication
- The way that we say what we say, which accounts for 36% of the communication

You can see from this that your body-language is a massive influencer of the whole communication piece and therefore extremely important in how you use body-language in an interview. Also, the way that we say what we say is also very important, so again we need to be mindful of this at interview. Let's just try and put some meat on these very important bones.

Body-Language

Even if you're feeling nervous, try not to show it. Fidgeting, fiddling with your hair or anything else you know that you do when nervous are all things that you need to keep under control, and let's face it, it's only going to be for an hour or so.

Whatever your height – tall to small and anything in between, stand tall with your shoulders back and head held straight, particularly when you first stand up to meet the interviewer. Smile a warm and genuine smile and make sure your hand-shake is a good solid firm one – but please, not so firm that it crushes the other person's hand, and definitely not limp-wristed so that it feels like the person is shaking hands with a wet fish - Just enough firmness for both to feel comfortable.

Eye contact is important. There is nothing worse than speaking to someone who averts their eyes away from you, or looks past you when they are speaking to you, so don't do it. When the interviewer is speaking to you, look them in the eye and answer them clearly, confidently and succinctly, using the preparation techniques we discussed earlier.

Positive Impact Body Language at Interview	Negative Impact Body Language at Interview
• Open and warm approach • Firm and confident handshake • Sitting and standing straight with shoulders back • Smiling warmly and sincerely • Making regular eye contact • Varying voice tone, pitch, pace • Head held upright or	• Cold and distant approach • Limp handshake • Hand crushing handshake • Miserable or worried facial expression • Slouching (either sitting or standing) • Fidgeting, playing with hair or hands • Grinning (as opposed to smiling)

slighted tilted • Enthusiastic and positive voice	• Not making eye contact (can be perceived as 'shifty' or having something to hide) • Speaking in a monotone voice (no variance of tone, pace or pitch) • Voice too quiet or too soft and difficult to hear (could be perceived as lacking in confidence • Folded arms (can indicate defensiveness) • Bowing head forward (can be perceived as shyness or nervousness) • Staring (can be perceived as aggression)

Overall, as far as body-language goes, just adopt an open, relaxed and professional approach that conveys an air of balanced confidence. Now by balanced confidence I mean, not so confident that you come across as arrogant, and not so humble that you come across as shy or laid back – A balance between respectful humility and confidence is exactly the right mix.

The Way That You Say What You Say

This is really about your voice tone, pitch and pace. If you've ever heard yourself speaking on a recording you will know what your voice sounds like. If you haven't, why not give it a try, just to gauge what you sound like to others, but I warn you you'll hate it, most people hate the sound of their own voice. The reason it's a good thing to do, is so that you can experiment with just injecting some variation in tone, pitch and pace from time to time. If this is way out of your comfort zone and is freaking you out just thinking about it, then don't worry, talking in a subtle, confident tone will be really effective - just try to sound enthusiastic and positive, that will work just fine.

The Words That You Use

While the words that you use only account for 7% of the communication they are still important, particularly at interview as the interviewer will be hanging on to, and probably making notes, of everything you say. So in conjunction with your body-language and the way you say what your say, they have an important part to play. Below are some High and Low Impact Words and Phrases to be mindful of:

Positive Impact Words and Phrases at Interview	Negative Impact Words and Phrases at Interview
- Of course - Yes I agree - I'd be delighted to - Yes - Let me give you an example - Definitely - Absolutely - That's not a problem - In my experience	- Can't - Won't - Impossible - Maybe - Perhaps - I'm not sure - I don't know - I don't have an example - I can't comment on that

Making an impact is essential if you are to be successful in getting the job, so we need to make sure that for the duration of the interview at least, we become our own public relations officer. Remember what we said earlier: at interview you are in your own shop window, so this is absolutely the time and the place to be at your very best in every way, in every detail and leaving nothing to chance.

> **Please know and understand that employers are becoming more and more discerning about the quality and calibre of people they employ. The penny is finally dropping that employing the wrong people costs money, both in lower productivity and therefore profit, and also in repeat advertising and recruitment costs. You want a prospective employer to be certain that they're making the right choice in employing you. To do that, you have to make a great impression, you have to be credible and believable, and you have to have prepared fully and comprehensively in the way that we've described.**

The Clothes That You Wear

The clothes that you wear to your interview speak volumes about you and who you are. You may not think what you wear is that important, but trust me it is. Put yourself in the interviewers shoes, and imagine someone turning up for interview in a shabby suit or dress that looks like it's never been near an iron, or someone wearing a tie with yesterday's lunch splattered down it, or wearing a shirt or a blouse with sweat marks around the neck.

Believe me all of these things have happened to me as an interviewer, and as good as these people may have been, they never got the job. You see, my reasoning is that if someone cares so little about their appearance that they can turn up for an interview in that state, then how much care will they take over their work? – Answer? Not much. There are no circumstances that would get me to employ someone who turned up for interview in this way no matter how well they interviewed. You might think this is unfair, but believe me most interviewers would think this way.

Clean well pressed, smart and appropriate clothes is what is required – and don't forget to polish your shoes. You may not think clean shoes are important but you'd be wrong. A shabby pair of shoes can spoil the whole image of a person, and if the interviewer is an ex forces person, the impact of dirty shoes will be even more profound.   If you look the part, you'll feel the part.

Personal Grooming

I know it's obvious, but trust me there are some people who think it's OK to turn up for interview with greasy hair, dirty fingernails, nicotine stained fingers, dirty teeth, garlic smelling breath (from the curry the night before) and so on. Forget it - you'll be dead in the water before you know it.

You Are Your Own Unique Person – There is No-One Else on This Earth The Same As You.

This is a fantastic fact of life and one that can really help you get any job you want. The best and most influential tool you have at your disposal is you. Because an interview is a platform for choosing the right employee you can exploit your strengths and personal qualities for all they're worth. But in order to do this, you have to know what they are, which is why the preparation is so important.

You have to stand out; you have to communicate through every sinew of yourself that you are absolutely the right person for this job. You are selling yourself to your prospective future employer, so this is your chance to convince them of your worth.

What is it about you that makes you unique and different to everyone else on this planet? Is it your great personality, your warmth, your generosity of spirit, your positivity, your energy, your confidence, your sense of humour, your quick brain and intellect, your voice and accent, whatever it is, exploit it. These are your natural talents – use them, this is no time to hide your light under a bushel.

However, one word of warning, any strength over done becomes a weakness, so remember exploit your strengths, but don't go overboard, because you'll have the opposite effect.

Part 2

Part 2

OK The rest of this book is dedicated to those who have a little more time to spend honing up on these important skills. I trust those of you who may have had imminent Interviews have benefited from Part 1 of this book. If you have you'll already know how powerful being prepared is to landing that all important job.

In this section, I will cover some of the remaining topics that will support your endeavours to get that all important job. Part 1 of this book is ideal for those who don't have much time and need to move quickly, however, Part 2 will provide a broader and more rounded knowledge of the complete Recruitment process to help you get that job.

As a reminder there is a Contents list overleaf:

Part 2 Content

Your rights and entitlements under Redundancy	*103*
Writing your covering letter	*113*
The recruitment structure	*121*
Telephone Interview	*121*
First Interview	*123*
Final Interview	*124*
Panel Interview	*125*
Psychometric testing	*129*
Assessment activities	*133*
The inexperienced interviewer	*149*
Confidence	*151*
Assertiveness	*175*
Marketing yourself	*181*

Your Rights and Entitlements under Redundancy

First of all many people ask: "Is Redundancy the same as dismissal?" The answer is that Redundancy is a form of dismissal, and usually the reasons for someone being made Redundant will be one of the following:

- The need of the business to reduce costs, often resulting in staff cuts (the cost of employment is one of the biggest overheads most businesses carry).

- The job that you held is now surplus to requirements, and is no longer required.

- The business you work for is moving location, or is closing down.

- New systems or technology have rendered your job superfluous.

When someone is made Redundant, they should expect their employer to behave with integrity and at the very least the following procedures should happen:

1. You are entitled to be selected for Redundancy fairly.

2. You should be 'consulted' about the Redundancy prior to it being formalised.

3. You should receive any Redundancy pay that you are entitled to.

4. You should be afforded the correct amount of Notice.

5. Alternative to Redundancy should be considered by your employer.

So let's have a look at each of these in a little more detail:

1. You are entitled to be selected for Redundancy fairly:

    There are numerous 'reasons' that employers use for Redundancy, the main ones of which are as follows:

- Last in – first out (this is simply the employees with the least amount of service that would be selected).

- Self selection, where your employer asks for volunteers for Redundancy.

- Appraisals, skills, experience, qualifications.

- Disciplinary record.

Occasionally employers use a combination of one or more of the above within their selection criteria, and often this would involve a scoring system of some kind to aid the selection process.

Also, employers may deploy a selection process that requires people to apply for their own jobs as a means of helping them to select for Redundancy. It is usually not mandatory to apply, and in either case, until you are formally notified that you have been selected for Redundancy, and then made Redundant, you are still employed.

When Selection is Perceived to be Unfair

You have the right to appeal your employer's decision to make you redundant if you feel that the selection was unfair. This would normally be in writing and stating your reasons, with your views of what you believe your employer should do to right the situation. If the matter goes to an Employment Tribunal the manner and method of selection will influence whether the tribunal considers the Redundancy to be fair or not.

You cannot be selected for Redundancy on any of the following grounds:

- Membership of a trade union (or non-membership)

- You are a female on maternity leave

- You have disclosed information about your company's wrongdoing

- You have reported your company for Health & Safety breaches

- You have or are about to attend jury service

- Any other reason that is deemed to be discriminatory

2. Consultation

   Ordinarily there are two methods of consulting staff for Redundancy; collectively; or individually.

   Collective consultation:

   If there are 20 or more staff members that are planned to be made Redundant (within a 90 day period), you or your elected representative should be consulted before notice of Redundancy is served.

   Consideration by the employer should be given to the alternatives to Redundancy together with ways to reduce the impact on those people who are selected (skills training might be an example of this), and it should take place within 30 days of the Redundancy taking place – or 90 days if 100 or more staff members are involved.

   If your employer fails to comply with these requirements, you are entitled to take your employer to an Employment Tribunal, and may be awarded up to 90 days of pay by way of compensation.

Individual Consultation:

An 'individual consultation' will require your employer to consult you directly and providing the reasons that you have been chosen for Redundancy together with any alternatives to Redundancy that may exist for consideration

3. Redundancy Pay

If you have worked for your employer continuously for a period of two years or more you are entitled to receive Redundancy pay which is not subject to taxation. This rule also applies to fixed term contracts of two or more years that do are not renewed because of Redundancy.
However, if your employer is successful in finding you suitable alternative work and you refuse this work, you no longer retain the right to be paid Redundancy pay.

If you are laid off from work for more than four consecutive weeks you are entitled to claim Redundancy pay; also if you have been laid off for six weeks in any thirteen week period.

The calculation for Redundancy pay is based on the following:

- Your length of continuous service

- Your weekly pay (current legal limit is £330 at time of publication)

- Your age

Specifically, the entitlement to Redundancy payment is as follows:

- If you are below the age of 22 years, you will receive half a week's pay for each year of continuous service.

- If you are above the age of 22 and below the age of 41 years, you will receive one full week's pay for each year of continuous service.

- And finally, if you are 41 years or above, you will receive one and a half week's pay for each year of continuous service.

- Above the age of 65 years, there is no entitlement to Redundancy payment.

In all of the above circumstances, your employer should provide you with a written statement of how your Redundancy payment has been calculated. If you are unhappy with either your payment or the way it has been calculated write to your employer asking them to correct the situation. If you remain unhappy and if they fail to respond in the way you believe they should you do have redress to an Employment Tribunal, however, you should note that you have six months from the date of Redundancy to make a claim.

4. Alternative Work

- If you have been consulted for Redundancy, and your employer offers you alternative work prior to making you redundant, they need to provide you with enough information about the alternative work to enable you to make an informed decision. In other words you need to know how it differs to your current job: does it require additional or different skills? Is the pay and benefits different and by how much (more or less)? What are the hours of work? Where is the job located? And so on. These are also the things that will determine if the alternative work offered is 'suitable' or not.

- If you have secured alternative work with a different employer prior to the date of your Redundancy, you may want to request your current employer to release you early. Most reasonable employers are happy to do this, given the circumstances. If however, they refuse your request and you leave anyway, you run the risk of them not paying you either some or all of your Redundancy pay. You can still appeal the decision not to pay you, but get advice first. (See Addendum No. 2 at the end of this book for list of place you can gain further advice).

- If you have two years continuous service by the date of your redundancy (date your notice period expires), you should be allowed by your employer a 'reasonable' amount of time to look for alternative work and attend interviews with an alternative employer. This will also apply to organising training or skills development. There is no 'black and white' definition as to what is deemed to be 'reasonable' however, this should be discussed with your current employer to ascertain what they believe is 'reasonable' in these circumstances.

10

Writing Your Covering Letter

You may be tempted to think that your covering letter is just something you throw together just a couple of minutes before you either pop your CV in to the post, or zip it down the line on email, and you'd be wrong.

Your covering letter is the first thing that the CV Sifter will see, even before they've had chance to look at your CV. You may have spent hours labouring over every detail of your CV, shaping, honing and tailoring it precisely to the requirements of your proposed employer, only to lose out because you didn't spend enough time on your covering letter, and it hasn't 'hooked' the sifter or worse still it contains something that has raised a concern with them.

OK, that said, let's get in to the guts of what a covering letter should contain.

Whether by post or by email it's always good advice to keep your covering letter in accordance with formal letter-writing conventions in relation to format and style, so for example: Name of Person to whom the letter is addressed at top left of the letter, together with the name and address of the company. Your own name and address should go to the top right of the page. If you applying in response to an advertisement, use the specific reference and/or job name in the Subject or Reference line, so that it is clear which job you are applying for, and embolden it, or underline it, so it stands out. If you are applying unsolicited, I will cover this a little later, but for the purposes of this section, I am assuming you are responding to an advertisement.

In terms of the format of your letter, it should follow the same principles of all good marketing letters, after all that's what this is – a personal marketing letter, so, for example: your first paragraph should hook the Sifter in and encourage them to read on; your second paragraph should expand on the first and provide the Sifter with succinct, pertinent and relevant additional information designed to both inform and influence them about your credentials for this role. Please be mindful of the word 'succinct' – it is important to keep your letter to about 1 side of A4, but to make every word in it earn its place on the page. Your third paragraph should provide a brief summary and an expression of your desire to be considered for the job. A re-emphasis of how delighted you would be to be given the opportunity to attend for interview.

The following is a sample of a covering letter that would be considered by most to be a high quality covering letter:

Paul Smith
23 Edmonds Drive
London
WS1 2NQ

Miss Rebecca Clarey
HR - Recruitment Department
Technology Services Ltd
Salmon Drive
London
W1 9PY   1st February 2009

Dear Miss Clarey

Ref: Job Reference No. 298 – Vacancy: Logistics Manager, Harrow

I write in response to your advertisement in the London Gazette on Thursday 28th January and have enclosed my CV as my application for the position of Logistics Manager at your Harrow site. I would also add that I have long followed the fortunes of Technology Services Ltd and in terms of values, culture and ethos it is my view that I would be a good business fit for your company.

I have been in Logistics for the past four years, and have gained extensive experience managing complex logistic systems for our company over the last 18 months. I currently manage a team of 8 people across 2 sites, the activities of which span the length and breadth of the United Kingdom. I am an active 'self developer' and continuously strive to be not just an effective Manager to my team, but also an Inspirational Leader. Logistics is not just a job to me it is something I am passionate about and spend a lot of time studying the very best logistic operations; how they work, and what makes them successful. I am 100% ready for the next stage of my career and I would be delighted if that is with Technology Services. I have won numerous awards at my current company and strive always to be the best in whatever I do. I do have very high performance, behavioural and attitudinal standards, as do my team. I have actively groomed an excellent successor to take over from me in my current role and therefore feel that I would be leaving my current position in very capable hands.

I would be delighted to be able to explain further why I believe I am a strong candidate for the position of Logistics Manager at Harrow and how I can add real value to the role at Technology Services Ltd. Thank you for your time today.

Now I trust it is evident why it is a good example of a covering letter. However, let me expand a little further on the reasons:

In the first paragraph, the writer mentions values, culture and ethos and how he believes he would be a good fit for the Technology Services business. This is excellent as he is indicating that he has an understanding of the company's values, culture and ethos, and yes this is likely to be questioned and discussed at interview, but it tells the interviewer (and Sifter) that this is someone who has done their home work. Add to that the statement that they believe they would be a 'right fit' for the business, and this is a powerful first paragraph that is definitely succinct but would encourage the reader to read on.

In the second paragraph; this is really the meat and main thrust of the letter. Its purpose is to influence and convey a compelling reason why the person should be considered for interview. It should be a powerful reiteration and support for the information that is contained in the CV (and remember they haven't read the CV yet).

What it should not do is regurgitate the content of the CV – I've seen this done so many times and it's a big mistake. They're about to read your CV so they don't need to read the same content twice; this will only serve to irritate. So this paragraph needs to contain supporting, but compelling information that you haven't included in your CV.

So how does our sample letter stack up against this? Extremely well is the answer. Consider the following: such as the fact that he is passionate about logistics (it isn't just a job), and that he studies logistics as a subject together with the best and the most successful logistical operations, and he has managed complex systems. This is good copy and every word has earned its place in that letter.

There is also the information about his very high standards in relation to behavioural, performance and attitudinal considerations, and that of his team also. This is great information to put in a covering letter. The other compelling pieces of information are: the fact that he has won many awards; he has groomed a successor to take over from him when he leaves (very powerful statement); and he is 100% ready for the next stage in his career, which he wants to be with Technology Services Ltd.

Every word in this paragraph has been carefully crafted for maximum impact and would definitely create a positive impression in the eyes of the Interviewer

Sifter. Of course it is worth mentioning that your CV has to be just as compelling and powerful, but a covering letter akin to the one outlined earlier is a fantastic start.

So, just to recap:

- Your letter needs to follow traditional letter-writing conventions in terms of layout and format.
- It should be no more than one side of A4 paper.
- It can be typed or written, either is fine – but make sure it is legible.
- 3 paragraphs only.

- Every word needs to earn its right to be on the page.
- Paragraph 1: Hooks the reader in and mentions something about the company that you have found out in your research (values, culture, ethos).
- Paragraph 2: Compelling and powerful additional information that is not contained in the CV (or not contained in the same way, but might be referred to).
- Paragraph 3: A reiteration of your desire to work for the company and to have an opportunity to expand on the reasons you believe you are the best person for the job, and a thank you for their time.

11

The Recruitment Structure (Telephone Interview; First Interview; Final Interview)

The Recruitment structure can differ from business to business, so I will outline here the likely stages that many companies follow. Not all companies use every stage e.g. telephone interview, but some do, so it's worth covering these here.

The Telephone Interview

This is becoming more prolific as a first-stage screening tool in more and more organisations, particularly where time is at a premium. It therefore makes perfect sense to conduct an initial interview over the telephone; perfect sense for the company that is, but it does also mean that you as the applicant are put at a distinct disadvantage because all you have at your disposal is your voice, and if you're not that comfortable being interviewed on the phone, or you're aware that your voice is a little monotone (even boring) then you won't come across as impactful as someone else with a great voice tone, pitch and pace. The good news however, is that you can learn the skills of voice projection, but it does take practice, and is beyond the realms of this book. So for the purposes of this book, let's focus on content.

The main purpose of a telephone interview is to screen applicants for those that will be put forward for interview, so only those that perform well against set criteria will get through. It is important therefore that you come across as credible and as polished as possible. If your voice skills aren't great, you will absolutely need to ensure that your content is extremely good, to stand a chance.

Now you will need to assume that the Interview could take up to about an hour (they can take longer, but this would be unusual). You need to prepare in exactly the same way as for the main Interview, so one and the same activity, you don't need to do it twice. It's likely that you will be asked some of the main questions that will be asked at the main Interview, if you are lucky enough to get through.

A telephone interview is usually shorter than a main interview (around half an hour is most common) although as we've said it can be up to an hour. In view of this, you will need to make sure you get as much of your key information across in an appropriate way. Now by 'appropriate way' I mean to subtly weave your key information in to your answers. In other words try to provide information over-and-above that being requested.

This is a powerful technique to use and is subtle. Most applicants would usually just provide the information being asked, and not think to weave in the additional information. This is particularly important in a telephone interview because if the Interviewer doesn't ask the question, and you only provide the information they ask for, all the great information you've prepared won't get aired, and you may not get through to the next stage. You really can give yourself an enormous advantage if you do this as you can be sure most of the other applicants won't.

First Interview

Some businesses choose to hold more than one face-to-Interview. Once again, this is another stage of the screening process. Usually, only those candidates that have been short-listed, usually no more than three candidates, will be invited back for Final Interview, so this is a critical stage in the process, as are all the stages. The same degree of effort, care and preparation needs to go in to every stage of the process. The first face-to-face interview is your gateway to a potential final interview, so you have to perform to the very best of your ability.

The first interview is likely to follow the process outlined earlier in Part 1 of this book and may be based upon a competency framework interview structure.

Final Interview

This is likely to be the toughest stage of the interview process and this is because you are probably one of only three or four candidates, and you will all have been chosen because you have all deemed to be the applicants who have most closely matched the selection criteria for the role, so you will be benchmarked against other strong candidates. This is the time to keep your nerve and keep the pressure on yourself to do the very best you can.

At this interview there are likely to be additional elements that were not included in the first interview. Whereas the first interview is likely to establish right fit for the job, the final interview will likely want to establish right fit for the business, so could include interview questions around values, work ethic, personality traits; also psychometric testing and a series of assessment activities. A section on psychometric testing and a further section on assessment activities is included later on, so I will not regurgitate these here.

Panel Interview

This type of interview can seem a little daunting however you should see it as an opportunity to have a favourable impression on even more key decision makers within the organisation. Remember, you've prepared thoroughly, you've anticipated the questions you may be asked and you've prepared your answers, you've got all your key information firmly in your head and you know how to weave it in to your answers, even if the question doesn't get asked. You're ready.

A panel interview is just a number of people (it could be as many as eight people), who have been asked to be part of the interview process for the role usually because the role in some way impacts upon the panel members' parts of the organisation, or because the organisation believes it to be a more robust method of recruitment. At this stage the reason is irrelevant, just look upon it as an opportunity. Given your preparation, you won't fail to impress at least some of the panel, if not all.

There is another reason why panel interviews are a positive and that is because if you aren't successful for the role you applied for, you have effectively been interviewed by a number of people and you are now 'on file' for all of those interviewers who may have been really impressed by you, and will want to keep you in mind for any openings they may have in their departments in the future. So, when you walk in and see four people looking back at you think of it as four opportunities, because that's exactly what it is. Again, most candidates will see this as another hurdle and a barrier to them getting the job. You really can turn this in to a genuine advantage.

Just a cautionary note: Please be sure to direct your answers to all the panel members, not just the person who asked the question. This will show respect and that you understand that they are all part of the decision making process.

Should I Ask Questions at Interview

This is an interesting stage of the interview. It is at this stage that both you and the interviewer(s) have now formed some opinions – you of the organisation, the role and the interviewer, and your perspective of how things have gone, and the interviewer(s) on how you stack up against the criteria for the role and an overall impression of your strength of application and suitability for the role. By this stage you will already have been getting an overall impression of how it has been going – trust me, interviewers are human and no matter how professional they are, if you're not doing well, you'll be receiving some subtle messages (body language, facial expression, voice tone etc) so be 'aware.'

Conversely, if you're doing well, the same applies – you'll be picking up those positive vibes too.

Towards to end of the interview, it is normal for the Interviewer to ask if you have any questions. If you haven't done particularly well, they may instead say something like: "We'll be happy to answer any questions you may have at the next stage of the process if you get selected." I know this sounds unfair, but it's just a fact of life. Interviewers are human, and if you haven't done well, they're hardly likely to want to spend a further ten minutes answering questions about the organisation, the role, or terms and conditions. On the other hand, if you've done well, or they believe you could be the person for the job, they'll usually invite questions from you.

If they ask the question, please don't say "No, I don't have any questions." This could be seen as lack of interest, even though that's not the case or your intention. Have a least two questions, but not lots of them – three or four is about the most you should have at one interview. You can always save the rest for when (and if) you receive the job offer. These could be questions about the organisation, or clarifying questions about the role or terms and conditions.

Psychometric Testing

Many organisations use psychometric testing as part of their recruitment structure, particularly for key roles, such as management, sales executives or customer facing roles. This type of testing is a useful method of indication that supports the interview process. Often the psychometric test is conducted prior to the interview as it will usually provide areas to probe at interview and also suggest some key questions to be asked.

Psychometric tests are usually constructed around two main themes – personality and intelligence. There are many testing tools on the market today, far too many to list, but if you google 'psychometric tests' you'll see the myriad of tests available. Some web sites allow you to take 'sample tests' on line free of charge, and it is a really good idea to do this so that you get a sense of how they work. You will usually get a sample report back which could act as invaluable feedback prior to an interview. Most of these tests operate around what are known as 'norms' which are the cumulative results of literally thousands of people which are measured to create a 'norm' i.e. the level at which the majority of people have scored. Scores above or below are reported as being outside of the 'norm' either a strength or a development area and cited within the report as an area to probe at interview.

Psychometric tests are not used exclusively for recruitment they are also used for development purposes to highlight key areas for development and can also be used to support Training Needs Analysis (TNA), also for team development.

The tests which focus on personality are usually based upon something which is referred to as the Introversion – Extraversion scale and is deemed to be an indicator of personality traits. Probably the best known of these is the Myers Briggs test.

Tests which focus on Intelligence (IQ) are a very useful indicator of the levels of ability someone has. Again these should be used as support information for the whole process and not based on this alone, so you can only hope that this is the case with your prospective employer. In view of the nature of these tests, you need to ensure you are alert as these tests will require you to answer within a set time limit. Whilst they measure predominantly Intelligence they also measure speed of thinking, so you really do need to be on your mettle.

The more practice you can get with these types of tests the better and the more able you will be to control your nerves on the day. Some people who have never taken a psychometric test before completely go to pieces when they are confronted with the test; their mind goes blank and they are frozen by the sheer fear of going through this process. Don't let this happen to you. Do as many of these free tests as you can beforehand so that you're not completely thrown on the day.

That said, the results of psychometric testing, should never be the sole source on which to base a recruitment decision, as it is purely an indicator. The risk for you as the applicant is that if you have a poor and inadequate interviewer, they may be tempted to rely more on the psychometric test than on the interview. This underlines the need for you to ensure that you get your key information across at interview, no matter how poor and inadequate the interviewer is. If they're not asking the questions, you have to find a way of getting your information aired and discussed. Most applicants won't do this, so you'll be giving yourself the best chance, and hopefully the results of the psychometric testing will support this.

Assessment Activities and What to Expect

Assessment activities are an additional element of the recruitment process which many organisations adopt. Once again it provides the organisation with additional information about your suitability for the role for which you are applying. Activities will vary but will have been designed to test you in a live scenario to see how you perform 'on your feet.'

The activities included will be dictated by the role and will vary in relation to the role applied for. A Management position for example might have a different set of activities to say an Administrative role. What follows are some typical activities that most often appear at Assessment however bear in mind that the content of the activity will vary depending on the role.

Presentation:

These can take various methods of brief. Sometimes you will be given the subject matter on which to present and the brief will be quite specific about what is required. Sometimes, the brief will be quite fluid and loose and in this case the requirement will be to see how you interpret the brief.

Occasionally you will have no prior knowledge of what the assessment includes and you will be required to create the presentation there and then before presenting it to the Assessor(s), or you may be given the brief before hand to prepare your presentation before you come. If the brief doesn't say, you should check if there is a preference for the presentation to be on power-point or flip chart. If there is no preference and this is left to you, go with what you feel more comfortable with. Power-point does look more polished than flip chart, but if you're not familiar with this method of presenting stick with flip chart, as it is content that is most likely to be of more importance.

A simple structure for your presentation is the following:

- Tell them what you are going to tell them – Introduction and Agenda
- Tell them – Main body of your presentation
- Tell them what you have told them – Summary and Conclusion

The main body of your presentation should also have some structure to it and should 'flow' in the way you present it. The following is an example of a structure that can be used if you are being asked to present on any subject that requires you consider a future position. In a nutshell: you should first outline the topic at a top-line level; then how it relates to the current situation; then consider the options available; then finally the proposed way forward. This follows a very simplistic model of GROW, which stands for:

G-oal	What do you want to achieve – i.e. the future position?
R-eality	Where are you now – what is the current situation?
O-ptions	What choices or options do you have available?
W-ay Forward	Which of these options do you propose to move forward with?

Of course it will depend upon the brief and subject matter as to whether this simple model is appropriate. It may not be, but do make sure that you work to a structure.

Case Studies:

These activities are favoured where it is required to establish perhaps the scope and depth of an applicant's thinking and how they apply that thinking to the role. A Case Study activity usually replicates a given scenario which has a number of facets and considerations to it.

It is more common for case study activities to be used with 'white collar' roles so will not normally be required in blue collar assessment activities, although not exclusively.

There are many variations on the Case Study theme. The type and style of the Case Study will be determined by the nature of the role. They can range from reasonably simplistic Case Studies for more junior office type roles, to quite sophisticated Case Studies for Senior Management and Director Positions.

However, what they will all require is a degree of analysis of a number of pieces of information that will need to be considered in terms of their relevance and importance to the task (and the brief). You may also be asked to prioritise your findings in relation to how they rank on the Urgent/Importance scale. Occasionally some 'red-herring' information is also included that you will need to identify so that you can separate it from what does need to be included in your presentation, which will usually be to one or two assessors. Sometimes, Case Study activities are not required to be presented but take a written format given in to be marked by an assessor later, which is worse as you don't get an opportunity to explain your thought process. In these circumstances you absolutely have to ensure you get all your rationale down on paper, so that it can be easily followed and understood by the assessor.

Having been involved in both creating Case Study activities and marking them, I can assure you that lots of people do not make it clear on paper what they mean and what their rationale is.

As an example, in Business Case Studies where a Senior Manager is required to analyse say six or seven pieces of information about a business, so perhaps a set of Management Accounts, a list of Key Performance Indicators (don't worry if you don't know what these are, a Senior Manager would), some information around customer loyalty, some marketing statistics providing market share; penetration and segmentation data, and perhaps a profile of the business and its key managers. Let's imagine that the brief for this is as follows:

'Consider all of the information provided and conduct a full and comprehensive analysis on this business. There are at least six key points of importance in each division of this business that the assessors will be looking for you to identify. Your written report should contain your findings; conclusions; and recommendations.'

Now this is quite a loose brief and will be open to much interpretation by the applicant about what is relevant, urgent, important, and what is not. However, this is quite common in very senior positions as the task will be attempting to ascertain the depth and scope of the applicant's thinking, their ability to think strategically as well as operationally, and to convey this in writing so that it makes sense to the reader (the assessor).

The applicant would be given a set amount of time for this activity, and given the scale of the brief, would normally be around three to four hours.

A real tip here is to always try to provide the assessor not only with your analysis evaluation of the Case Study but also (time permitting) with some risks and opportunities. Also because there is a financial element to this, you will need to quantify your recommendations so that it is explicit what result your recommendation will bring to the business. So for example: if you are recommending that Sales Volumes are increased by 10% by doing 'xyz' quantify what 10% increase in volume will mean in financial terms, so your written recommendation might look like the following:

Finding:

The sales volumes of Widgets in the 'abc' market is significantly below its direct competitors and other Widget divisions within the group. From the information provided it would appear that this is because the 'abc' market has not had any marketing focus or investment for the past 2 years. In previous years when marketing and headcount resource was present the penetration and volumes were at least 10% higher than they are today.

Conclusion:

The poor result in both Widget sales volumes and 'abc' market penetration can be attributed to a direct lack of investment in marketing and resource investment. The costs associated with marketing and resource (using previous years' statistics and applying an index linked factor of 3% year on year) have been estimated at approximately £9,500.

Recommendations:

Increase Sales Volumes of Widgets by 10% by increasing penetration of the 'abc' market. This will result in an additional £65,400 in turnover, £35,000 in Gross Profit less additional costs of £9,500 which will produce a Net Profit of £25,500. The calculation for this is as follows:

10,000 Widgets x 10% = 1000 x £6,540 per Widget = £65,400 less COS £30,400 = £35,000 less marketing and resource cost of £9,500 = £25,500 Net Profit. This would provide an improvement to the ROS (Return on Sales) of an additional 2%, and ROFE (Return of Funds Employed) by 0.2%.

So what I'm advocating here is to quantify all your recommendations in quantitative terms. This will let the assessor know that you understand the actions you are proposing and that you have considered them in quantifiable terms. If the above recommendation was just:

Increase Sales Volumes of Widgets by 10%

The assessor would be left wondering what rationale was being used to arrive at that recommendation and what difference would that make to the business. Always think of Case Study analysis activities as 'end result' activities. For sure the assessors will be wanting to see your objective thinking clearly demonstrated, but they will also want to know that you know the end result impact of your recommendations on the business overall and you can only do this by quantifying them.

In-Tray Exercises:

The above is a 'high level' example usually used for Senior Managers and Directors. For more junior positions say Administrators, P.A.s, Office Managers, Junior Managers, Clerks etc. A more simplified version of a Case Study might be used. These are often referred to as In-tray exercises.

Again, there will be a host of information presented to you which you will be required to consider and analyse. Where In-tray exercises differ is that they are usually created to establish 'prioritisation' skills rather than analysis skills of the Case Study. So you will need to look at everything you have been given and establish its priority in relation to the brief you have been given.

A great tip here is to use the 'time management' Urgent / Important Matrix model to help you with this, but just in case you haven't heard of this I'll outline it below:

Urgent	Important - Not Urgent
Urgent - Not Important	Not Urgent or Important

You can easily draw this for yourself during the activity to help crystallise your thinking and to help you categorise which information falls into which category. However, once again you will need to substantiate why you believe the information falls into the category you have suggested.

Always read through all the information provided first. Then go through it again, this time high-lighting and categorising as you go through. Try also to identify any information that may be related to another piece of information and any references that may suggest that something is dependent upon something else happening first. An example of this might be a piece of information that says that your boss has to be at a meeting in Europe, let's say Paris, next Wednesday and that travel arrangements have not yet been organised. In another piece of information it states that there is an embargo on travel expenses outside of the UK to attend meetings unless all other methods of being involved in the meeting (i.e. video conferencing, or audio conference call) have been ruled out as being inappropriate. The type of meetings that would be accepted for travel outside of the UK would be financial meetings where attendance via video conferencing would not be appropriate.

In this case, your priority would be to establish what type of meeting your boss is attending and this would need to happen prior to you making the travel arrangements for his trip. Most In-tray exercises include these kinds of related pieces of information, so you do need to look out for them.

People Development Activity:

These can take a number of guises however these days will usually be focused around the ability to Coach your people. This will mainly be for Managerial or Team Leader roles.

Ordinarily, this activity will be a scenario where you are asked to play the role of a Manager who is about to meet one of his employees who has some specific issues – these are usually performance or behaviour issues (rather than personal). The brief will provide an outline of the issues and will ask for you to conduct the meeting in your usual style and approach given circumstances such as these.

You will need to demonstrate your ability to coach and the observer(s) will be looking for how you approach the brief with this in mind. Some companies will tell you explicitly that they are looking for a coaching approach, but others will not, choosing to provide the brief and expecting you to interpret the approach that would be required in those circumstances. Adopting a coaching approach is a safe bet here in any case. The only caveat to this is if the brief is quite clearly more of a Performance Management or Disciplinary brief in which case more of a directional approach may be more appropriate.

Group Activity:

Most of the activities and exercises on Assessment Selections are individually focused and therefore most Assessment processes will also include an activity where you are required to be part of a group. Mainly this is to see how you interact within a group environment. This isn't just for Managerial roles but can be for any role that requires group or team interaction. The role that you have applied for will obviously dictate the brief for the activity but I will outline a few briefs that are typical from my own experience of running assessment centres.

1. Managerial

    As a group you will discuss the subject of 'The Importance of Customer Loyalty' and present back (to the observers) your key thoughts and conclusions from your discussion.

Let's be frank here, the subject matter is almost immaterial as usually the main focus of the observers will be to see how well you conduct yourself in the interactions with the other members of the group. They will be looking for how well you communicate, to what degree do you contribute to the discussion - do you encourage the input of others in the group as well as your own? Do you dominate or are you willing to listen to the views of others. How well do you accommodate the others views that may be different to your own? Do you talk over people in order to make sure you're heard, or do you allow other more dominant members of the group to take over – neither of which will gain you any points on the scoring grid?

The key is to adopt a balanced approach being neither too dominant nor too quiet. Demonstrating active listening and acknowledging others input is desirable. Assertive but not overly is ideal. Arrogance is never an attractive quality and true leaders also have a healthy modicum of humility.

The mistake many managerial candidates make is that they mistakenly believe that in order to show their Leadership skills they have to lead and dominate the discussion. This is a big mistake and only goes to show how misinformed they are and how lacking in Leadership ability they are. Leading the discussion is fine to a point as long as you involve and encourage the other members of the group. If yours is the main voice being heard you won't be giving the best impression. Keep it balanced.

Other Group Activity Examples:

2. Administrative

    As a group discuss and present back on the balance between detail and bigger picture tasks, and how to prioritise these.

3. Sales

    As a group discuss and present back on adherence to sales process and the occasions that you might need to step outside the process in order to make the sale.

4. Sales – Mobile

    As a group discuss and present back on: the merits of cold calling.

Recap of Final Interview Activities

You can begin to see how all these elements combine to provide the interviewer and organisation with a rounded and comprehensive perspective on you the candidate's suitability for the role.

Sadly, some organisations only apply one element, the Interview, to their recruitment process and these are usually the organisations that suffer performance management issues further down the line. It is 'high risk' to base recruitment decisions on an interview alone and businesses that do this leave themselves vulnerable and exposed. However, that's not your problem - all you can do is respond to whatever the process entails.

If you know you don't perform well at psychometrics and/or assessment activities this could work in your favour, but it could also indicate an organisation that is less than ideal. If it doesn't take its recruitment seriously then what else might be amiss in the organisation? What is the calibre of its people and managers? What is its overall performance like? I personally would have serious doubts of any organisation that only had Interviewing as its whole recruitment process. You may think that's unfair, but my experience tells me otherwise.

Studies have shown that there is a direct correlation between the rigor and robustness of a business's recruitment process (or not) and its business results (Return on Investment, profitability, customer loyalty, staff retention, to name but a few). Why? Well the stronger the recruitment process, the higher the calibre and quality of people recruited, and the higher the propensity for those people to perform well, which in turn impacts directly on business results.

The Inexperienced Interviewer

Unfortunately there are some pretty poor Interviewers in this world and these are also the people who are tasked with employing great people for the business they represent. Someone once said to me that businesses get the people they deserve, and I 100% agree with this. We don't let inappropriate characters in to our homes but when it comes to our business it seems that its open house. Where businesses have HR departments and support this tends not to be the case, as usually they will provide the training, direction and tools to Management to make sure they adhere to the recruitment process. It is normally in smaller businesses where this support function is not in place that problems arise.

As stated earlier on the face of it, this is not your problem except that you may be interviewed by one of these inept, incompetent people. Whilst it's never going to be the most rewarding experience to have to go through you can still do a great job of the interview by making sure you get in all of your preparation information.
It will be pretty evident when you are in front of someone like this, and that's fine, you just need to stay alert and focused and ready to slip in your key information

when you get an opportunity. Sometimes you will encounter an Interviewer who dominates the air-time, and goes on and on and on. You'll just have to wait until he/she stops talking so that you can weave in what you've prepared. It might sound awkward and it may well be so, but you might as well make the best of a bad job (Interviewer) and at least leave knowing that you gave it your best shot.

Confidence

You may be surprised to know that you were confident once. Yes, every person on this earth was born confident. As a baby when you were hungry you didn't even think about demanding to be fed, you just opened your lungs and your demands spilled out, or when your nappy needed changing, same thing. When we're born we don't have any of the negative behaviours that adults gain along the 'life road' we're just us. There'd be no point anyone telling us we're useless or wouldn't amount to anything at that age, because it wouldn't make any difference, we'd probably have gurgled right back. We'd be too young to understand.

As a baby we are at the truest time of our life. Truest in the sense that we are 100% who we are, straight from our Mother's womb, unconditioned, unbridled, unaffected, perfect in every way. It is only as we become aware and begin to make sense of the world that 'who we are' begins to be affected by the people and situations that surround us as babies and children.

As we grow, our personality is constantly being shaped by our experiences and the people who are with us in those experiences. Experiences range from euphoric to traumatic and everything in between, either way many experiences stay with us for many years, if not for ever, particularly those at either end of the range – euphoric and traumatic.

It has been scientifically proven that experiences that touch our emotions at a very deep level stay with us. Even if at a conscious level we have no clear memory of a traumatic experience, our unconscious mind will have stored it and packed it away. Our in-built defence mechanisms are very adept at shielding us from traumatic memories by filing them away in our unconscious and vast filing system, so that we don't have to re-live the experience day in, day out. Traumatic memories can stay buried for many years, but often they resurface and usually at a point where we can better handle the emotional velocity attached to them. The resurfacing can be triggered by all sorts of different, seemingly innocent events; a piece of music; a smell; an article in a newspaper; a person's name; something you hear someone say; it could be anything, but when it happens it's like the opening of Pandora's box and all those buried memories comes flooding back.

Mental illness apart, it is possible to get back to a 'true' state and way of 'being' that is as close to the real and true you as it is possible to get. Every negative thing you have been conditioned to think about yourself over the years, can be unlearned and unconditioned, you just have to want it enough. You cannot change the experiences, but you can change the impact they are having on you, just by changing your thinking. I promise you and guarantee that if you really want it badly enough and are prepared to put in the effort to achieve it, you can be the person you want to be. I've seen it happen too many times to have doubt.

Too many people have suffered unbelievable adversity and lived not only to tell the tale but to help many people to learn from their experiences. Louise Hay, now a famous American author, experienced unbelievable physical and sexual abuse as a child and young girl, and then later ovarian cancer and not only did she come through it, but out of her desire to help others, through her books she laid bare her experiences to the world to help those who could benefit from knowing how she got through it. Now in the autumn of her life, she is very much still an active leader of the Hay Foundation and has helped thousands and thousands of people around the world. Her book Heal Yourself is definitely worthy of reading. Both her book and Louise have inspired me greatly.

Children in an 'unconditioned' state are without fault or flaw. The early years of a child's life are its most formative. Children learn at a phenomenal rate, taking in thousands of pieces of new information and new experiences every day. You were no different. As a child the majority of your learning happened up to the age of 5 years. Think about it, you learned to walk, you learned a whole language, you learned how to read body language, how to get what you want, that's no mean feat for a 5 year old, but you did it and probably quite effortlessly. Unfortunately during this time you were also beginning your journey of 'conditioning' so called because at some point along the way, we begin to learn the rules of the life game. We learn about the things we mustn't do; the things we mustn't say; about danger and bogey men; the bad people and not to speak to strangers; about manners and politeness; about being good little children; about caring and relationships; the birds and the bees; death and heaven; about life.

We also become 'conditioned' by our experiences and as already stated; these can span the spectrum from euphoric to traumatic and everything in between. We already know that the memory of emotional negative experiences stay with us, albeit often 'filed' away in our unconscious mind. However, the experience hasn't just created a memory, it has also helped to condition our senses to recognise the symptoms and characteristics of a potential similar experience happening. Have you ever felt extreme unease or a feeling of trepidation in a situation where everyone else is fine and your feeling is without any real foundation. Even you don't understand it, yet you know that you feel that way but you don't know why. The answer probably lies somewhere in your unconscious mind, something about the situation is awakening deeply held and deeply buried feelings that is causing a heightening of your senses. Even if your conscious mind doesn't remember, your unconscious mind is being triggered by what your eyes and body are seeing are experiencing at a conscious level. Everything in our unconscious mind can only be accessed via our conscious mind.

What does that mean, I hear you saying? Well simply, everything in our unconscious mind gets there through being filtered through our conscious mind. Our mind is in two parts conscious and unconscious. Everything that we experience every day gets filtered in our conscious mind and those experiences don't just go away. After a few days, if we have not revisited the experience either physically or in our thoughts, i.e. brought back to consciousness, then it moves out of consciousness and into unconsciousness; our enormous personal filing system. Now when a similar situation or experience presents itself to us, our conscious mind goes searching for anything in our filing system (unconscious mind) that will help or support our understanding of what we are now experiencing and bring it back to consciousness.

It's like some smells can evoke images in our mind of something or situation the smell reminds us of, and immediately that previous experience of when we last experienced that smell is right there with us in the here and now. It could be anything: a smell, a piece of music you hear on the radio; a song; someone you meet that reminds you of someone else; a situation; anything.

Have you ever found yourself harbouring a complete dislike of a particular name? A dislike that goes way beyond just personal preference; I mean an absolute hatred of the name. Well in all probability, this is because that name is the name of someone you held that same level of dislike for, and as human beings we transfer this dislike of the person to the name they hold also. So every person we subsequently meet with that same name, we unconsciously associate the characteristics of the previous person that we didn't like to this new person that we are meeting for the first time. Yes it's irrational and without logic, but that's how our mind works. It's a sort of defence mechanism that goes back to our cave dwelling days.

I hope you're beginning to realise how complex we are. Complex but perfect too. You see because everything that is in our unconscious mind in filtered through our conscious mind, this means that we can retrain our mind to serve us better.

Let's take a live example of someone who became a client a couple of years ago. Paul was a neighbour of mine and the son of a lovely couple who were really friendly and helpful. Paul lacked confidence and had a low self esteem. He described his life as "a catalogue of disasters" and that "nothing ever went right for him." Paul in fact was a very talented computer programmer – self taught. He believed himself to be in his words "a waste of space." When I asked him why he referred to himself in this way, he told me that this is how his father often referred to him, and had done all his life. It was a surprise that Paul had got to work with me in the first place; I had bumped into his Mom out shopping one day and mentioned that my printer seemed to have died a death, and she kindly said she would ask her son Paul to have a look at it for me.

I'd often seen Paul coming and going, but had never before engaged in conversation with him. He seemed really shy and it was evident that he found conversation with me a really uncomfortable thing to do. After a while, just passing small talk about my printer and what was wrong with it, and how he was putting it right, he became a little more comfortable. When I thanked him for fixing my printer I asked him what he did for a living, expecting him to say he was some computer programmer or something similar. What he told me floored me. He stacked shelves at the local supermarket. My face probably spoke volumes in that split moment. I apologised immediately, but followed this by asking him why a talented individual such as him is working at the local supermarket stacking shelves. I've never seen anyone blush more in my life; he went crimson. I again apologise and told him that I hadn't meant to embarrass him, but that I was still really curious as to why. Anyway, he agreed to have a cup of tea with me, and we just chatted. When he talked about computers and all things techie, his complete physiology changed. His eyes came alive. He became expressive and it soon became evident to me that this young person in front of me was not living his best life.

He had no real friends and he said he'd got used to being "a bit of a loner" which he told me he didn't really mind that much, as he found most of the guys he worked with shallow and boring. I asked him how it would feel to work with like-minded people who shared his love of computers. Again his face lit up, and he just answered "that would be great, but it'll never happen." "Why?" I said "Because I'd never get that sort of job, those jobs are for clever blokes."

Now Paul was with me for a good two hours, so I'll spare you with all the details, but suffice it to say that I took Paul through a process of bringing all the negative thoughts he had of himself into consciousness and helped him see that he was choosing to believe these distorted stories about himself that weren't true. The person he had described could never have fixed my printer for me, and definitely couldn't programme computers. So he was believing a whole pack of lies about himself because that's what he'd always done, and no-one had ever shown him a different way until that day. I helped Paul believe that if he chose to, he could be the person he longed to be.

Over the subsequent 12 months, Paul embarked on a college course for computer programming which he sailed through, got a couple of qualifications under his belt and I coached him on all the techniques on how to successfully get through the job finding process, but the job he passionately wanted above all else.

He eventually applied for and got a job at an IT Consultancy company as a junior programmer. He also signed up with the Open University to do a degree in Computer studies. Being in a job he loves, surrounded by people who share his passion has completely transformed that lad beyond recognition. He even has a girlfriend, something he had told me he didn't believe he'd ever have. He met her as a fellow Open University student. Paul is following a different path and has *chosen* to live a different life, rather than let life dictate and control how he lives his life.

I bumped in to him a couple of months ago, and asked what the relationship with his Father was like now, and he just smiled at me, then said, "well it's been a long time since he called me a waste of space, and we even went for a pint together a few weeks ago."

All I did with Paul is help him 're-programme' (forgive the pun) his thinking and to see that he had a choice. The way that he was living his old life was of his own making, he just didn't realise it was of his own making. I helped him see that he was unconsciously hiding behind his father's seemingly low opinion of him, and using this as a excuse not to move forward. He was wallowing in his own imagined misfortune and in a strange sort of way he enjoyed it that way.

"It is always easier to live in the past or the future than to confront the present."

What this means is that some people find comfort in wallowing in their own misfortune, they blame everyone but themselves for the situation they are in – their Dad, their Mom, their Boss, their Teacher from years ago, anyone as long as *they* don't have to take responsibility for what has happened to them.

They adopt an 'I'm a victim' mentality, 'please feel sorry for me, it's not my fault, you see my Dad died when I was 11.............." or "my Dad told me I was a waste of space all my life" or "my Mom was a single parent and we never had any money" or "my Teacher said I'd never amount to anything" I hope you're beginning to see a pattern here. Yes, this is victim mentality language.

Paul was 100% in this mode of thinking. In order to change his life, he needed to move his thinking out of the past (his Dad telling him he was a waste of space) and out of 'I'm a victim' mode. I helped him see and feel what a different life could be like and encouraged him to imagine his life in that new and different way. He could choose a different way if he wanted it enough. He did, but he was just 'stuck in the past.' He'd got used to living his life in a particular way and hadn't ever allowed himself to even consider there could be a different way.

Once he realised he did have choices and that he was in complete control of his own life, he made the most important decision of his life. That decision has changed his life and he is now blossoming into a confident and assured young man, who knows where he's going and what he wants out of life - My goodness what a transformation.

It's a Mind Thing:

If I tell you that where you are today, is as a direct result of the choices you have made in your life so far, how would that make you feel. Well whatever your feelings, it is a fact. We are all in direct control of our own destiny. The bad news is we can't change the past. The good news is that we can change the future.

I meet so many people who come to my workshops and tell me how life has been so cruel to them, and what bad luck they've had in their life, and it is these things that have created their current situation of being broke, unhappy, not enjoying their work and so on, and so on, and so on. And I say "It is you that has chosen to be broke, unhappy and not enjoying your work. You can make a different choice if you want to, but you have to want it enough."

Well I can tell you right now these people are just a tad shocked at my approach, but it certainly gets their attention. I genuinely want them to learn this stuff, and therefore I have to tell it as it is, and how I see it. Cruel, cutting, ruthless, maybe, but if it gets them to look at themselves differently, it is worth it.

In the world of psychology, there is a state which is known as 'victim syndrome' and the situation described above is absolutely a symptom of this. You know those people who spend their entire lives living in the past, wallowing in their own misery, recounting their bad luck stories over and over again to anyone who will listen.

What's really sad about these people is that they tell themselves these stories too, and even worse they believe them. I have many clients who when they first come to me for help, they are in this very negative state. Once I have listened very patiently to their tales of woe I acknowledge what they have said, and then ask them to describe their future. They really struggle with this, because they are so used to thinking and talking about stuff that has already happened. They fill their heads with their hard luck stories of this problem and that bit of back luck, all true I hasten to add, but still taking up every bit of available space in their head.

Then I ask them to imagine themselves driving a car whilst constantly looking in their rear view mirror, rarely glancing at the road ahead of them. What would happen if you did this, I ask. At this point I usually get a slight smile. "No really" I say, "concentrate on what I'm saying, what would happen if you did this?" "I'd crash" they say. I think you're getting the point by now, and so do they. If you spend your life in the past, the rest of your life will reflect exactly what your past consisted of. If you stay in victim mode, you'll spend your life being a victim. What's more worrying is that whatever we focus on, we tend to get more of. So constantly thinking about the awful things that have befallen us, just opens the floodgates for more awful things to pour in.

Now let's just think for a short moment about something I've just said, and that is: "what we think about, we tend to get more of." At an unconscious level, we are predisposed to the things we think about most. This is where the term 'self-fulfilling prophecy' came from. You see as human beings what we fill our minds with, we have a tendency to bring in to our lives. It's about focus – you see we're wired to bring about what we focus on, so when we focus on the negative stuff in our lives, we tend to get more of it. When we focus on positive situations and positive self-talk, we significantly reduce the opportunity for negativity to come in to our lives and increase the probability of good things in our lives.

Some pretty eminent and powerful people have been saying this for centuries - just have a look at a few of the following quotes from them:

"Whatever the mind of men can conceive, it can achieve." – Clement Stone.

"Imagination is everything - it is the preview of life's coming attractions." – Albert Einstein.

"Whether you think you can, or you think you can't, either way you are right. – Henry Ford.

So, for the third time, what we think about, we get more of. Please, please, please, do not think for one moment that this is just about positive thinking, it isn't, its about so much more than this.

A big mistake some people make is that they resolve not to live their life in the past, - good start, but then they start living their life in the future – not good. What do I mean by this? Well their dreams, wishes and aspirations remain just that – dreams wishes and aspirations. Phrases such as: "One day I will…….., " or "I am going to be…….," or "when I get………." are all future-tense phrases. People get really skilled at imagining and dreaming about their future, about their 'one day' scenarios. This is fine as long as they are taking action today towards that future. If not it will always remain a dream, never to be fulfilled.

Let's get a little deep here. Imagine dying at a grand old age and never having achieved your full potential. In fact let's make this come alive. Imagine you have always dreamed of having financial freedom, a partner and children that love you dearly and who you love and care for and can provide a good and fulfilling lifestyle for, and a job that you were so passionate about, you just loved every minute of it.

However, imagine that you never achieved any of this, and you died frustrated, in regret, and full to the brim of unfulfilled dreams and wishes. So you get to the gates of heaven and an Angel tells you that before you can enter the Kingdom of Heaven, you have to meet the person you *could* have been if you had fulfilled your full potential on earth. You meet this other you and you are immediately in awe. The 'other you' shows you a visual of their life on earth and all the great things they achieved. You see your friends and family all influenced and impacted so lovingly and positively by your life. You see your children at your eulogy speaking about you in such wonderful glowing terms; they talk of the difference you made to so many people's lives. How you helped so many people get on in their life and how your love for your family wrapped its warmth around all of them. They spoke of the legacy of love, wisdom and laughter that you left your children and how they would take this forward in their lives for their children, and their children's children. They spoke of your hard work ethic and determination to be the best that you could be, and how you never gave up even when you failed, which you did many times. They said you were the greatest role model they could ever have, and they hoped their children to come would love them as much as they loved you at this moment.

If you had died, and this exact scenario happened, how would you be feeling right now? Take a couple of minutes to think about that. Who would you meet at the pearly gates? Would you meet an exact replica of you today, or someone you always dreamed of being, but didn't take the action required to be that person? Ask yourself this question, what would it take for you to become this other you? What would you need to do differently today to achieve this?

Well this brings us nicely to the point. Live your life in the present. Live with intention, and remember to move your legs, i.e. take action. You can't change your past, but you can change your future, how? - By working on your 'present.' Refuse to live in a dream bubble for one moment longer. Burst the bubble and make it happen. Take what you want in your future, and write it down now. Seriously, do it now, write what you want in your future right now. Let your imagination run riot.

I'm assuming that getting the job you want and are passionate about is part of that future; it might even ultimately be owning your own business. Write it all down now. The very process of getting your thoughts, dreams, hopes and aspirations out of your head and down on to paper is the first step towards taking action.

Now take the most important of the things you have written down and think about what you would need to do to make that become a reality. What's the very first step you would need to take? Write it down.

Often you won't know what these steps are, and it might be that the very first step might be to do some research and find out some information, that's great and it is taking action. You probably won't be able to write down the next step until you have done the research, that's fine too, just make sure that you do take the research action. You'll find as you take each small step, the next step will become obvious to you. There is a wonderful saying which I've always found to be the case, and that is:

"When the student is ready, the teacher will appear."

I love that saying simply because in my own experience I have found it to be so true. Whenever I have not known what to do, I adopt the principle of 'just do something' and pretty soon, just by doing something, the next step shows itself to me. This has happened to me too many times in my life to be a coincidence. Try it, you too will see that once you do something, the next step will show itself to you.

It's when you do nothing that nothing happens. Nothing shows itself to you when you are inert.

Many people don't take action because they are in fear – fear of failure, fear of making themselves look stupid, fear of change and so on. Fear is a terrible 'state' that we allow to control our lives. There is a wonderful book called 'Feel the Fear and Do It Anyway' by Susan Jeffers and it captures the essence of fear so well.

Fear is a defence mechanism that we all have within us and evolved over time in human kind to keep up safe. When we are in danger we feel fear which puts us in to a 'fight or flight' state of mind. It prepares us to react and respond quickly to dangers we may encounter in our lives. The flip side of this is that we have developed our sense of fear so well that if not controlled it can stop us doing and achieving so many of the things we spend our lives dreaming of.

The feeling of fear itself is an uncomfortable feeling. Our nerves and senses are heightened and it's as if our whole body goes in to 'red alert' mode (fight or flight). Now of course if we are in danger, this is exactly what we need. However, often times people feel fear in lots of situations where they are clearly not in physical danger, but they perceive themselves to be in emotional danger, which is why the feeling of fear kicks in.

Let me explain: Public speaking or doing a presentation in front of a number of people can harbour huge feelings of fear for many people. They are not in physical danger but they fear they won't be able to do it, or they'll forget their words, or they'll make themselves look stupid. This is a perception of emotional danger. I say perception because it is exactly that – it is an imagined danger. We conger up in our mind all sorts of disasters happening; we play it in our heads as if it were real. We see ourselves stumbling over the words and we see the audience looking on unsympathetically; we feel the shear embarrassment and humiliation of the moment and then we 'run a mile' metaphorically speaking. Wild horses wouldn't get us to get up and present after the experience we've just played out in our mind. That's how fear can work against us in this context, and I'm sure we're all familiar with something similar to the above happening in our lives.

Fear *is* real, it *is* an uncomfortable feeling but it doesn't mean we always have to adopt the 'flight' reaction. Sometimes in that heightened state we should try to adopt the 'fight' response, which is to accept that this is going to feel uncomfortable but that you are going to conquer the fear by doing whatever it is you're afraid of.

You know when someone has a fear of something it stays with them all their lives until they eventually conquer the fear by doing the thing they are scared of doing. Only then do they lose that fear. How disabling and how sad is that - Going through life with a fear that haunts us and is ever present lurking permanently at the back of our minds controlling us like an invisible force.

Our fears can only survive if we feed them. Every time we give in to a fear, we feed it, and we make it stronger. Every time we conquer a fear we disable it and make it weaker, eventually eradicating it altogether from our lives.

Accept that fear comes from our imagination; we imagine ourselves failing and that's what creates the feeling of fear. The good news is that if we can imagine ourselves failing, we can also imagine ourselves succeeding. You need to practice this skill over and over again. Whatever it is you are fearful of, you need to play the scenario in your head of you succeeding time and time again, until the scenario is so familiar to you, even you would have a problem even thinking you could fail. Trust me this approach really works. It's what the best athletes do prior to their race; they imagine themselves running their race and coming first and they replay that over and over in their head. It's what the best golfers do, the best swimmers, the best presenters, the best negotiators, the best business people, the best everyone. You name it, the best in any category you care to mention all practice this principle. It is no accident that they are the best at what they do?

What can you learn from this? Imagination is enormously powerful and hugely underestimated in its control of our lives. It is seeing a scenario in your mind that hasn't happened yet and you are the director of the film, you can make it a happy ending film, a cliff hanger film, a thriller, or a disaster film – the choice really is yours, but whatever film you choose to play in your mind, studies show that there's a really good chance of that film or scenario becoming a reality. So get good at only allowing positive scenarios to play in our minds. If you find yourself entertaining negative imaginations, replace them with a positive scenario immediately. Replay it over and over in a positive way and a positive outcome until it feels real.

Why am I telling you all this, and what has this got to do with getting a job? Well many people have a fear of interviews and they play the interview over and over in their mind; they see themselves doing really badly and then being told they haven't got the job. They mistakenly believe that if they tell themselves this, it softens the blow when it actually happens. This process is flawed and what it actually does is create a self fulfilling prophecy. It is precisely because they have played out the doomed scenario that they are most likely to make it happen in reality.

You really can imagine yourself in to a job. It's the next best thing to actually being at the interview for real. You're imagining the interviewer making you feel at ease, and you're feeling a little nervous but very well prepared and confident. You see yourself looking polished and smart and impressing the Interviewer. You can hear the questions the Interviewer is asking you and you can hear your response which is clear, concise and again making a really good impression – you can see the Interviewer nodding her head while you are speaking and smiling as if in agreement with you. You're feeling good and really enjoying the experience. Whatever happens you know you're making a favourable impression and that you've given the very best that you can give and that's all you can ask of yourself.

If you did this over and over until you were so familiar with the scenario you could recount it word for word, there's a high possibility your actual experience would be a really positive one. No of course it wouldn't reflect your imagined scenario exactly but you'd stand a really good chance of being at your very best in terms of preparedness and ready for whatever came up at the real interview.

THIS IS POWERFUL – PLEASE TRY IT FOR YOURSELF!

16

Assertiveness

Assertiveness is about living your life in balance and about being as close to the true you as you can be. Assertiveness is a way of behaving that speaks volumes about who you are as a confident person. Please do not confuse assertiveness with over-confidence or arrogance; assertiveness is neither of these. It tells people that you are in control of your life and living a balanced and fulfilling life.

The good news is that assertiveness is a learned behaviour it is not a trait, so anyone can choose to become assertive, they just have to learn how to do it. This is a great skill to demonstrate to any prospective employer.

To become assertive may require some hard work as you may need to change some deeply held beliefs, perceptions, habits, and ways of being that you have so far always adopted in your life. These can be changed but you will need to put in some effort to achieve this.

A fundamental shift in the way that we behave day to day is what being assertive will require. What I mean by this is that it will require real focus. Let's just start by explaining where our behaviours come from.

How we behave is driven by how we think, and how we think is driven by how we feel, and how we feel is driven by what is known as a 'trigger event' – something that happens or something that someone says that evokes a feeling within you. These are considered 'external' events however it is here that these external events can sometimes link directly to our deeply held beliefs, perceptions and habits. You see we all interpret external events by how we see the world. If our experience of the world to date has been a negative and bad experience, we can tend to interpret everything that happens to us as negative, no matter how positive it actually is and no matter how much people tell us that it's positive. If our 'inner voice' (unconscious mind) doesn't believe it, we will automatically filter the information we are getting and interpret it as negative.

We all have two 'inner voices' a negative one and a positive one. Our in-built defence mechanisms predispose us towards developing our negative inner voice to protect us from hurt of failure – if we don't try we can't fail right? Well yes, but that's also what keeps people living in victim mode. So the trick here is to develop a more active and louder positive inner voice. This is what will require most of the effort. You have to start thinking positive thoughts about yourself and absolutely not believing all the negative things your negative inner voice will be telling you such as: "you're not good enough" "you can't do it" "there's no point trying, you'll fail" "you're a waste of space" "you're not good enough" "you're not worthy|" and so on.

These negative interpretations are just that; interpretations of deeply held beliefs that have evolved over all the years of your life, but you need to know they're not true. Our unconscious mind tends to believe what it hears repeatedly (either from yourself or others) as if it is true, then it holds that belief as a distorted truth that shapes everything else that happens to us, so if someone tells us we're good at something, and we've previously held the belief that we're useless, we'll most likely not believe the person, and choose to believe our negative inner voice, because the person couldn't possibly be right could they?

When you first start to develop your inner positive voice you won't believe what it's telling you and will want to believe the negative voice instead, but you have to control this. You won't be able to stop the negative voice coming in to your head, but you have to learn to make the positive voice louder and keep repeating in your mind positive thoughts about yourself. Remember what we said earlier: that our unconscious mind believes what it repeatedly hears. So in order to develop an active positive inner voice, you have to let your unconscious mind hear your positive inner voice talking repeatedly over and over. Eventually it will begin to believe what you are telling it, and when this happens you will truly be in the realms of life changing possibilities.

So how does all this link to assertiveness? Well as we said assertiveness is a learned behaviour and the first part of this is thinking positive things about you. Even though at first your unconscious mind won't believe what its hearing, over time it will as you repeat this positive talk over and over again. In the meantime you can become conscious of how you behave. Assertiveness is about being aware of our behaviour which should be acceptable to both ourselves and the people around us.

Aggression is a flawed and negative behaviour as is manipulation. Both can be perceived to get success quicker and in many cases this is true, but it is usually always at a cost, and that cost is also usually someone else's feelings and self worth. Aggression and manipulation are a symptom of insecurity and is born out of the need for power. Power feeds the ego, which in turn feeds the need to feel more 'secure.' In other words if we feel more powerful we also feel less insecure.

There are many advantages to behaving assertively namely:

- Feeling good about who we are and how we go about our lives
- Having other people respond to us positively
- Being able to shape your future by believing you can
- Being able to communicate our position more clearly
- Mistakes are merely opportunities to learn and to improve next time
- We are able to view criticism objectively and only believe if it based on fact
- Feeling happy in our own skin and proud of the person we present to the world
- Behaving appropriately at all times

Yes it takes effort and time, but the benefits are definitely worth it.

Assertiveness is about taking a rational and balanced approach and is fundamentally about controlling a situation so that both parties (or all parties) achieve a win/win outcome. Win/lose is not an acceptable outcome in assertion; aiming to keep the relationship intact and healthy is the priority. Avoiding conflict and arriving at a workable solution is crucial. Of course you won't always get what you aim for, but adopting an assertive approach to life will ensure you stay on the side of appropriate. You can't control how other people behave you can only control how you react to how other people behave.

Behaving assertively will allow you to express your strong feelings without losing control, or losing your temper. You will be able to communicate how you feel with clarity and to make your requests unambiguously rather than moaning and griping when life doesn't go your way.

Standing up for your rights without violating those of others is what assertiveness is about. It is recognising that although we have needs and rights, others have needs and rights also. An assertive person will strive to satisfy their own needs and wants whilst at the same time will strive for the other person's needs and wants to be satisfied also.

Marketing Yourself

You are your best marketing tool and your key influencer of others. How people perceive you will be determined by the you that you choose to show to the world. It is not enough to be good at something; you also need to be seen to be good at it. Everything you say and do tells the world who you are and what you stand for.

Taking responsibility for your own behaviour and your way of being in this world will be what influences other people to perceive you as either a good or not so good human being, or even a good or not so good employee.

At an interview you are not only selling your proposition as a prospective employee, you are also selling your personality. It is so important that you understand this, as both will be important to an employer. It won't be good enough just for you to demonstrate that you can do the job you have applied for, but also that you will fit in. Your personality will be coming through no matter how subtly and no matter how much you may be trying to be on your best behaviour. A skilled interviewer will have structured the interview so as to uncover key personality traits, and this might be accompanied by a personality profile also (psychometric test).

You are your own unique person, there is no person the exact same as you on this earth and you must get skilled at believing and living this truth if you are to become your own best advocate.

You are the sum of all the individual parts of you: your visual appearance, your voice (tone, pitch, pace, accent), your personality, your humility, your humour, your compassion, your positive outlook, your demeanour, your strength, your mental alertness – all of the things that make YOU. Be proud of you. Constantly strive to be that other you, you know the other you that achieves and takes action so that dreams become reality.

"You are your own unique person, there is no person the exact same as you on this earth and you must get skilled at believing and living this truth."

A Final Few Words from Doreen:

I hope that you have enjoyed this book as much as I have enjoyed writing it. More than this, I hope that you use it to get the job you want. Being prepared is always the key to confidence and confidence is the key to self esteem. You will need to spend some time preparing, but I promise it will absolutely be worth it.

I would really appreciate receiving your experiences and personal stories around this topic, particularly if you have put some of this in to practice and got the job you wanted as a result. My email address is doreenyarnold@blueyonder.co.uk Good luck with your new ventures, present and future.

All rights reserved. This material is copyright protected.

Copyright: It's About Results – All Rights Reserved
Publication Date: October 2008

www.ingramcontent.com/pod-product-compliance
Ingram Content Group UK Ltd.
Pitfield, Milton Keynes, MK11 3LW, UK
UKHW041437180426
11947UKWH00007B/495